廿一世纪全国应用型本科财经管理系列实用规划教材

外贸函电

主　编　王　妍　肖　艳
副主编　刘亚卓　梁志坚
参　编　李　涛　孟海樱　黄　伟

北京大学出版社
PEKING UNIVERSITY PRESS
中国林业出版社
China Forestry Publishing House

内 容 简 介

本书以外贸业务中的商务信函样信为例，介绍商务信函的写作方法、写作技巧，旨在使读者能够熟练运用英文，进行外贸相关业务的磋商谈判。本书共 12 单元，内容包括商务书信的结构和格式、询盘报盘和还盘、订货、包装、运输、支付、保险、索赔和理赔、代理、补偿贸易和加工装配贸易、寄售和易货贸易、合资和投标。本书所列样信既有原信，又有回复，每单元前面列有学习目的和教学要求，后面附有练习题以利复习和巩固，并在每单元后面列有与本单元内容相关的单据或相关的补充阅读或常用语句，介绍英文单据的形式和内容，信函中各种常用语句和表达方式以及其他相关文章。

本书既可作为高等院校财经管理类各专业的本科生教材，也可作为相关工作人员自学参考用书。

图书在版编目(CIP)数据

外贸函电/王妍，肖艳主编. —北京：中国林业出版社；北京大学出版社，2007.9(2009.9 重印)

(21 世纪全国应用型本科财经管理系列实用规划教材)

ISBN 978-7-5038-4884-1

Ⅰ. 外… Ⅱ. ①王… ②肖… Ⅲ. 外贸函电—英语—电报信函—高等学校—教材 Ⅳ. H315

中国版本图书馆 CIP 数据核字(2007)第 125009 号

书　　名：外贸函电
著作责任者：王　妍　肖　艳　主编
策 划 编 辑：李　虎
责 任 编 辑：苏玉辉　肖基浒
标 准 书 号：ISBN 978-7-5038-4884-1
出　版　者：中国林业出版社(地址：北京市西城区德内大街刘海胡同 7 号　邮编：100009)
http://www.cfph.com.cn　E-mail:jiaocaipublic@163.com
电话：编辑部 83220109　营销中心 83227711
北京大学出版社(地址：北京市海淀区成府路 205 号　邮编：100871)
http://www.pup.cn　http://www.pup6.com　E-mail: pup_6@163.com
电话：邮购部 62752015　发行部 62750672　编辑部 62750667　出版部 62754962
印　刷　者：北京中科印刷有限公司
发　行　者：北京大学出版社　中国林业出版社
经　销　者：新华书店
787mm×960mm　16 开本　10.75 印张　200 千字
2007 年 9 月第 1 版　2009 年 9 月第 2 次印刷
定　　价：20.00 元

丛 书 序

我国越来越多的高等院校设置了经济管理类学科专业，这是一个包括经济学、管理科学与工程、工商管理、公共管理、农业经济管理、图书档案学6个二级学科门类和22个专业的庞大学科体系。2006年教育部的数据表明在全国普通高校中经济类专业布点1518个，管理类专业布点4328个。其中除少量院校设置的经济管理专业偏重理论教学外，绝大部分属于应用型专业。经济管理类应用型专业主要着眼于培养社会主义国民经济发展所需要的德智体全面发展的高素质专门人才，要求既具有比较扎实的理论功底和良好的发展后劲，又具有较强的职业技能，并且又要求具有较好的创新精神和实践能力。

在当前开拓新型工业化道路，推进全面小康社会建设的新时期，进一步加强经济管理人才的培养，注重经济理论的系统化学习，特别是现代财经管理理论的学习，提高学生的专业理论素质和应用实践能力，培养出一大批高水平、高素质的经济管理人才，越来越成为提升我国经济竞争力、保证国民经济持续健康发展的重要前提。这就要求高等财经教育要更加注重依据国内外社会经济条件的变化适时变革和调整教育目标和教学内容；要求经济管理学科专业更加注重应用、注重实践、注重规范、注重国际交流；要求经济管理学科专业与其他学科专业相互交融与协调发展；要求高等财经教育培养的人才具有更加丰富的社会知识和较强的人文素质及创新精神。要完成上述任务，各所高等院校需要进行深入的教学改革和创新。特别是要搞好有较高质量的教材的编写和创新。

出版社的领导和编辑通过对国内大学经济管理学科教材实际情况的调研，在与众多专家学者讨论的基础上，决定编写和出版一套面向经济管理学科专业的应用型系列教材，这是一项有利于促进高校教学改革发展的重要措施。

本系列教材是按照高等学校经济类和管理类学科本科专业规范、培养方案，以及课程教学大纲的要求，合理定位，由长期在教学第一线从事教学工作的教师立足于21世纪经济管理类学科发展的需要，深入分析经济管理类专业本科学生现状及存在问题，探索经济管理类专业本科学生综合素质培养的途径，以科学性、先进性、系统性和实用性为目标，其编写的特色主要体现在以下几个方面：

(1) 关注经济管理学科发展的大背景，拓宽理论基础和专业知识，着眼于增强教学内容的联系实际和应用性，突出创造能力和创新意识。

(2) 体系完整、严密。系列涵盖经济类、管理类相关专业以及与经管相关的部分法律类课程，并把握相关课程之间的关系，整个系列丛书形成一套完整、严密的知识结构体系。

(3) 内容新颖。借鉴国外最新的教材，融会当前有关经济管理学科的最新理论和实践经验，用最新知识充实教材内容。

(4) 合作交流的成果。本系列教材是由全国上百所高校教师共同编写而成，在相互进行学术交流、经验借鉴、取长补短、集思广益的基础上，形成编写大纲。最终融合了各地特点，具有较强的适应性。

(5) 案例教学。教材具备大量案例研究分析，让学生在学习过程中理论联系实际，特别列举了我国经济管理工作中的大量实际案例，这可大大增强学生的实际操作能力。

(6) 注重能力培养。力求做到不断强化自我学习能力、思维能力、创造性解决问题的能力以及不断自我更新知识的能力，促进学生向着富有鲜明个性的方向发展。

作为高要求，财经管理类教材应在基本理论上做到以马克思主义为指导，结合我国财经工作的新实践，充分汲取中华民族优秀文化和西方科学管理思想，形成具有中国特色的创新教材。这一目标不可能一蹴而就，需要作者通过长期艰苦的学术劳动和不断地进行教材内容的更新才能达成。我希望这一系列教材的编写，将是我国拥有较高质量的高校财经管理学科应用型教材建设工程的新尝试和新起点。

我要感谢参加本系列教材编写和审稿的各位老师所付出的大量卓有成效的辛勤劳动。由于编写时间紧、相互协调难度大等原因，本系列教材肯定还存在一些不足和错漏。我相信，在各位老师的关心和帮助下，本系列教材一定能不断地改进和完善，并在我国大学经济管理类学科专业的教学改革和课程体系建设中起到应有的促进作用。

劉詩白

2007 年 8 月

刘诗白　刘诗白教授现任西南财经大学名誉校长、博士生导师，四川省社会科学联合会主席，《经济学家》杂志主编，全国高等财经院校资本论研究会会长，学术团体“新知研究院”院长。

前　　言

外贸函电是21世纪全国应用型本科财经管理系列实用规划教材之一，既是国际经济与贸易、商务英语、电子商务等专业学生重要的基础必修课，又是一门具有很强实用性、实践性和操作性的课程。本书顺应外贸企业日趋激烈的国际合作与竞争的形势需要，重点讲解外贸函电的基础知识和基础技能，旨在帮助读者在掌握外贸业务知识的前提下，能更好地运用英语技能，使他们将来在相关外贸的工作岗位上具备较强的适应性和独立工作能力，成为专业知识扎实、业务过硬、英语水平较高的外贸销售人员、谈判人员、管理人员等高素质国际复合型人才。

本书相对以往的函电类教材，具有以下特点：

1. 教学目标明确

每单元最前面都有明确的学习目的和教学要求，使读者易于掌握需要了解、需要掌握、需要熟悉的主要内容及相关内容。

2. 课文形式新颖

本书所列样信均“成对”出现，即既有原信又有回复，让读者了解在出现某种情况时采取何种语气、何种立场、如何措辞去写信，以及在收到对方此类信笺时应如何回复或应付，充分体现了实用性以及可操作性。

3. 课后内容与众不同

每单元后面均列有与本单元内容相关的单据或相关的补充阅读。相关单据旨在使读者了解单据，特别是英文单据的形式和内容，不仅要能看懂还要会填单；补充阅读包括本单元常用语句和相关内容阅读，使读者进一步增强外贸函电写作的应用性和灵活性，使读者扩大知识面，开阔视野，更好地理解有关专业知识和提高英语水平。

本书第1、11、12单元由上海杉达学院孟海樱编写，第2单元由莆田学院梁志坚编写，第3、9单元由兰州理工大学刘亚卓编写，第4、5、10单元由太原科技大学李涛编写，第6单元由辽宁工业大学王妍编写，第7单元由中南林业科技大学肖艳编写，第8单元由天津工业大学黄伟编写。全书由王妍作最后的整理和修订。

由于编者水平所限，书中不妥之处在所难免，恳请各位读者多提宝贵意见，以使本书日臻完善。

编　者

2007年7月

目　　录

Unit 1 Form and Structure of a Business Letter

Objective

- Understanding the essentials of business letter-writing
- Knowing the layouts of business letters
- Knowing the layouts of a business letter envelope

Requirement

- Get a knowledge of the principles of business letter-writing
- Grasping how to organize a good business letter
- Grasping how to address envelopes

Principles of Good Communication

A good business letter does not ramble on. It supplies all pertinent information in a clear and concise manner. Generally, Business writing has only two goals:

(1) To make people understand you.

(2) To get them to take proper action.

Your readers take the proper action only when they know not only what you say but what you want. Do you want them to:

(1) buy your product or service?

(2) confirm a decision?

(3) simply like you and think you are good to do business with?

All those things (buying, confirming, even liking and thinking) are actions.

In order to let your reader understand what you want (and then do it), he or she must first understand precisely what you mean in your writing. If he or she has to guess, there is a good chance the guess will be wrong.

People who read your letters have no opportunity to interpret your body language or tone of voice as they would in a conversation. So although you should write as much as you speak, you should think of the times when you speak at your best - when your words, sentences, and paragraphs are more precise than your typical everyday speech. Even when it is structured and precise, good writing helps your reader see you as a real person, and treat him or her as one too.

Time is valuable in business. Writing effective business letters will help you transact business quickly, effectively, and courteously. To write effectively, say what you mean, and make sure your readers understand you, keep the following principles in mind:

a. Clarity

Good business writing is all about being clear. The business letter should not have subtle allegorical overtones requiring careful study, or different shades of meaning. In short, it should not be open to interpretation.

Every word should mean one thing, each sentence should say one thing, and together they should create a tool for achieving your goal. Therefore, keep in mind the purpose of your letter and use appropriate words in correct sentence structure and convey your meaning. Good, what is needed for business letters straightforward and simple English is. If your reader understands you and does what you intend, then your writing succeeds.

b. Conciseness

Don't make your reader have to wade through long, rambling sentences. Write concisely and clearly and use a simple sentence structure. To achieve this, try to avoid wordiness or redundancy. Stick to your plan and only include information both relevant and necessary. Proceed cautiously here, however, because business writing should not be an endless series of short and choppy sentences. Don't be so concise that you become blunt.

c. Courtesy

Courtesy is not mere politeness. The courteous writer should be sincere and tactful, thoughtful and appreciative. It is the quality that enables us to refuse to perform a favor and meanwhile keep a friend; to refuse a customer's request for credit without killing all hopes of future business.

Another important thing is dealing with all letters promptly. Punctuality will please your customer who dislikes waiting for days before he/she gets a reply to his/her letter.

d. Completeness

A good communication should include all the necessary information. You should write not only what must be said, but also what should be said to achieve your goal. Make sure that your letter includes enough information for your reader to get what you mean, and that you come across as tactful and polite, not terse and unfeeling. It is essential to check the message carefully before it is sent out.

e. Concreteness

Strive to make your letter be exact, definite and specific, avoiding vagueness, ambiguity, or the use of platitudes. Most people use specific language when they talk casually：they tell stories with details, colors, and smells. Write in the same way. Use words to paint pictures in your reader's mind instead of letting him or her to dissect abstract concepts.

f. Consideration

Consideration emphasizes "You-attitude" rather than "We-attitude". When writing a letter, keep in mind the reader's requests, needs, desires, as well as his/her feelings. Try to understand and respect the reader's point of view and resist the temptation to reply as if you could not be in the wrong.

g. Correctness

Good business writing is correct in both technique and facts. Therefore, correctness refers not only to correct usage of grammar, punctuation and spelling, but also to standard language, proper statement, accurate figures, factual information and the correct understanding of commercial jargons. Again, check your letter over before you send it to avoid the awkwardness of correcting a mistake after your reader sees it.

the Structure of a Business Letter

a. The standard parts

A standard business letter contains seven parts: ① the letterhead, ② the date, ③ the inside address, ④ the salutation, ⑤ the body of the letter, ⑥ the complimentary close, and ⑦ the signature.

1) The letterhead

The letterhead expresses the personality of a company and often indicates the writer's company name & address, telephone number, fax number, email, internet website and the kind of business carried on. Usually it is centered or at the right or left margin of a letter writing paper. Nowadays, more and more business letters have preprinted letterhead stationary which contains the above information.

2) The date

The date is generally placed at least two lines below the letterhead to the right for indented style or to the left for the blocked style. The date should be typed in full and not abbreviated (i.e., November for Nov.) and the -th, -st, -nd and -rd that follow the day can be omitted (i.e., 3 May for 3rd May). Please see to it that the year is typed in full (i.e., 2006 instead of 06). Always spell out the month and include the day, a comma, and the year. The preferred forms of dates are as follows:

18 August, 2006　　　　August 18, 2006

Avoid giving the dates in figures, since it may easily cause confusion. It is English practice to follow the order of day, month and year while the American practice is to write in the order of month, day and year. So 10/6/2006 could be taken as either 10 June, 2006 or October 6, 2006.

3) The inside address

It consists of the correspondent's full name and address, which appears exactly the same way as on the envelope. It is typed single-spacing at the left-hand margin about two or four lines after the date. Generally, the inside name and address in a business letter should include the following:

(1) name of the firm or company addressed to

(2) number and the name of the building or house

(3) number and the name of street

(4) name of city, state or county and its postal code

(5) name of country

Ordinary courtesy titles used in correspondence are Mr. for a man, Mrs. for a married woman, Miss for an unmarried woman and Ms. for both married and unmarried women. In recent years it has become customary to use Ms. as the courtesy title for all women and many women, particularly career women, strongly object to being addressed as Mrs. or Miss.

Esq. instead of Mr. is sometimes used for certain classes of persons. Mr. always precedes the name while Esq. always follows the name, separated from it by a comma. e.g.

Mr. George Smith

George Smith, Esq.

Messrs., an abbreviation for the French word Messieurs, which is used only for partnership whose company name includes a personal element. e.g.

Messrs. S. Laurel and O. Hardy

Messrs. J. Waston & Co.

4) The salutation

The salutation is the polite greeting with which every letter begins. The customary formal greeting in a business letter is "Dear Sir (Madam)", "Dear Sirs (Mesdames)" or "Gentlemen", which is used in America. Do not use Sirs alone and Gentlemen can not be used in the singular. If the receiver is known to the writer personally, a warm greeting, "Dear Mr. /Ms. sb." is then preferred.

The salutation should be placed two lines below the inside address or the attention line (if used), and followed by a comma for "Dear Sir", "Dear Sirs", and a colon for "Gentlemen".

5) The body of the letter

This is the most important section of any business letter. Make sure that each paragraph is clear and concise. Start a new paragraph for each point you wish to stress and arrange the paragraphs in logical order so that your letter "reads easily" and moves, step by step, toward the aim or purpose you wish to achieve.

The first paragraph of a letter, mainly being a contact one, should usually be short. It may need to: (a) indicate the subject and the purpose of the letter, (b) acknowledge any previous correspondence, and (c) establish a satisfactory tone. The last paragraph should also be relatively short. It may: (a) show friendliness and good will, (b) leave the reader with a single clear-cut thought or idea, and (c) inspire whatever action or response is desired.

It is typed two lines below the salutation, or below the subject line, if any. In letters of average length, paragraphs are single-spaced and between paragraphs double-spacing is used. Very short messages may be double-spaced.

6) The complimentary close

The complimentary close, like the salutation, is simply a matter of custom and a polite way of closing a letter. Leave two lines of space after your last body paragraph, then place the close against the left margin (in fully blocked format), on the right or in the centre of the page (in letters which are in forms other than the full block).

The complimentary close should keep in tone with the salutation. The most commonly used sets of salutation and complimentary close are shown below:

Salutation	Close	Comment
Dear Sir(s)	Yours faithfully,	Formal
Gentlemen	Yours truly, /Truly yours,	Formal
Dear Mr. Harris	Yours sincerely, /Sincerely yours,	Less formal

Also notice that the close is always followed by a comma and only the initial letter of first word is capitalized.

7) The signature

A business letter should be signed by hand and in ink immediately below the complimentary close. The name of the writer is usually typed below the signature and most often includes the writer's title and/or professional designations. The use of a rubber stamp is a form of discourtesy.

b. the optional parts

The optional parts of a business letter are ⑧ the references, ⑨ the attention line, ⑩ the subject line, ⑪ the enclosure, ⑫ the carbon copy notation, ⑬ the identification line, ⑭ the postscript.

8) The references

The references number and letters enable the writer or the recipient to link the reply with the previous correspondence. The references may include a file number, department code or the initials of the signer of the letter followed by the typist's initials. They are placed immediately below the letterhead and marked "Your ref: " and "Our ref: " to avoid confusion.

9) The attention line

The attention line may be used if the writer of a letter addressed to an organization wishes to direct the letter to a particular member or department of the company. Flush with left margin or placed in the centre of the page, the line is generally inserted between the Inside Address and the Salutation, with double spacing above and below it.

10) The subject line

The subject line gives a brief introduction of the content of the letter, which is preceded by the word "Subject: " or "Re: " (Latin for "matter"). It is often placed two lines below the salutation and above the body of the letter.

11) The enclosure

It indicates that something else accompanying the letter is enclosed. Type the word "Enclosure" or an abbreviation of it (Encl.) at the left bottom with a figure indicating the number of enclosures, if there is more than one. If necessary, the enclosed documents or matters may be listed. For example:

Enclosures: 4

Encl. 3 copies of commercial invoices
4 copies of packing lists
Insurance policy

12) The carbon copy notation

When a copy of a letter is sent to someone other than the person addressed, type c.c. or C.C. two lines below the signature aligned the left margin, followed by the name of the recipient of the copy.

13) The identification line

The identification line shows the initials of the person who dictated the letter and those of the secretary or typist. The initials are usually typed two spaces below the signature against the left margin. The two sets are separated by a colon or a slant, with the dictator's coming first. The following examples are generally acceptable forms of the identification line:

BC: NB BC/NB MT: fjr MT/fjr

14) The postscript

The postscript (P.S.) is an afterthought, and in formal letter it is usually a sign of poor planning. Try to avoid the use of postscript as far as possible. If something is forgotten, it is better for the writer to rewrite the whole letter. If unavoidable, write in this fashion.

P.S. The invitation will be mailed to you in a day or two.

P.S. …to see you at the Annual Sales Fair at the Hillside Plaza on September 15.

(The Structure of a Business Letter)

1) Letterhead …………… …………….. 8) Our Ref. No. Your Ref. No. 2) Date 3) Inside Address 9) The Attention Line 4) Salutation 10) The Subject Line 5) Body of the letter …………………………………………………………………………… …………………………………………………………………………… ………………………………………………………….. 6) Complimentary Close 7) Signature 13) The Identification Line 12) Carbon Copy 11) Enclosure 14) P.S.

the Form of A Business Letter

Basically, the main styles of a business letter currently used are：① Full Block Style(平头式), ② Modified Block Style(改良平头式)and ③ Semi-Indented Style(混合式).

1) Full Block Style

Ms. Clara Winters
Jameson & Sons Ltd.
34 Madison Square
Melbourne B.C. 2
Australia
Our ref: EAS/CW
Your ref:

26 May, 2006

The Tiny Tots Toy Company
15456 Pyramid Way
College Park, FL 33133
U.S.A.

Attention: Mr. Raymond Simpson

Dear Sirs,

Re: Full Block Letter Style

The main characteristic of full block business letters is that everything (except maybe a preprinted letterhead) is flush with the left margin with no indention in the letter.

If your letter is only one page, type the complimentary close and optional components as shown below. Otherwise, type them on the last page of your letter.

Yours faithfully,

Jameson & Sons Ltd.
Clara Winters, Manager

2) Modified Block Style

Ms. Clara Winters

Jameson & Sons Ltd.

34 Madison Square

Melbourne B.C. 2

Australia

Our ref：EAS/CW

Your ref：

26 May, 2006

The Tiny Tots Toy Company

15456 Pyramid Way

College Park, FL 33133

U.S.A.

Attention：Mr. Raymond Simpson

Dear Sirs,

Re：Modified Block Letter Style

The main characteristic of modified block business letters is that everything is flush with the left margin, except the date, the complimentary close and the signature as shown. Modified block letters are a little less formal than full block letters.

Yours faithfully,

Jameson & Sons Ltd.

Clara Winters, Manager

3) Semi-Indented Style

Ms. Clara Winters
Jameson & Sons Ltd.
34 Madison Square
Melbourne B.C. 2
Australia
Our ref：EAS/CW
Your ref：

26 May, 2006

The Tiny Tots Toy Company
15456 Pyramid Way
College Park, FL 33133
U.S.A.

Attention：Mr. Raymond Simpson

Dear Sirs,

Re：Semi-Indented Letter Style

Semi-indented business letters are the same as modified block letters, except the paragraphs are indented and the subject line is centered. The inside name and address is typed in block form, while the date, the complimentary close and the signature are just close to the right of the center.

Yours faithfully,

Jameson & Sons Ltd.
Clara Winters, Manager

Addressing Envelopes

Envelope addressing calls for accuracy, clearness and good appearance. Business stationary ordinarily has the return address printed in the upper left corner of the envelope. The name and address of the receiver should be typed about half way down the envelope, which can be in the style of full block or semi-indented.

The postmark or stamps should be placed in the up right-hand corner, while the bottom left-hand corner is for post notations such as "Confidential", "Printed matter", "Certified", etc.

(Full Block Style)

China National Chemicals
Import & Export Corporation
Beijing, China

(stamp)

Messrs. William & Sons
T8 Lancaster House
Manchester, England

(Semi-Indented Style)

China National Chemicals
Import & Export Corporation
Beijing, China

(stamp)

Mr. F.M. Richard
c/o the Sales Manager
211 Broad Avenue
Los Angles, CA 91640
U.S.A.

Exercises

I. Arrange the following in proper form as they should be set out a letter:

(1) Sender's name: China National Lights Industrial Products Import & Export Corporation, Shanghai Branch

(2) Sender's address: 1001 Huangpu Road, Shanghai, China

(3) Sender's telephone number: 86-21-XXXXXXXX

(4) Sender's fax number: 86-21-XXXXXXXX

(5) Date: March 30, 2006

(6) Receiver's name: Jardin Matheson & Co., Ltd.

(7) Receiver' s address: 754 Craneigh Street, London S.E. 37, England

(8) Salutation: Dear Sirs,

(9) Subject line: 100% Cotton T-shirts

(10) Attention line: Mr. Simon Donnan, Import Department

(11) The message: We thank you for your letter of March 25 enquiring for the captioned goods. Enclosed please find the catalogue, which contains details of all our T-shirts and will enable you to make a suitable selection.

We are looking forward to receiving your specific enquiry with keen interest.

(12) Complimentary close: Yours faithfully,

II. Address an envelope for the above letter.

Unit 2 Enquiries & Replies

Objective

- Understanding and writing the letters connected with enquiries and replies
- Reading and understanding the relative documents

Requirement

- Grasping the usual usage of professional words and sentences
- Grasping the professional terms of orders

Introduction

Generally speaking, an enquiry is a request for information such as prices, quantities and other relative details about specific goods. It is usually made by a potential buyer, also called an enquirer. Sometimes, one regards enquires as the first step of a business negotiation. But, it is not necessary.

According to the content, Enquiries may be divided into two types: general enquiries and specific enquiries. If the enquirer wants to have a general idea of the goods which the addressee is in the position to supply, he may ask for a price-list, a catalogue, samples and other terms. This is a general enquiry. If the enquirer wants to purchase goods of a certain specification, he may ask the addressee to make a quotation or an offer for the goods. This is a specific enquiry.

When you write a general enquiry, you should first tell the correspondent how you get his name and address, state your intention of writing the letter and express your wish to enter into business relations. Certainly, if you are making a first enquiry, a brief self-introduction is necessary all the time.

Specific enquiries should be written briefly, concisely and completely. In general, writing a specific enquiry should concern the following points:

(1) What you are requesting for, such as the name and descriptions of the goods, a catalogue, a price-list and samples.

(2) A brief self-introduction and an introduction of market situation in your position.

(3) Asking whether there is a possibility of a special discount, what terms of payment and delivery time you would expect.

(4) Stating the possibility of placing an order.

(5) Show courteousness and politeness in your requests all the time.

Whenever you get an enquiry letter, you should make a prompt and careful reply. Reply letters answer questions, supply information and offer specific terms to satisfy the needs of the potential buyer. A reply letter should include:

(1) Acknowledging the receipt of the enquiry.

(2) Giving all the details of what you can supply and introducing the merit of the goods.

(3) Enclosing the catalogue, price-list and samples, which the enquirer requested for.

(4) Indicating the terms of payment and the possible time of delivery.

(5) Your wish to start practical transaction.

(6) Make sure you have answered all the questions raised by the enquirer, and include all the points you want to make.

Sometimes, you may receive an enquiry which you cannot satisfy at the moment, you should also acknowledge the letter immediately, giving the reason and assuring that you will do all you can to meet his requirements.

Specimen Letters

1. Request for Establishing Business Relations and Reply

a. Request for Establishing Business Relations

Dear Sirs,

We learn from our Commercial Office in your country that you are a large buyer of table-cloths. As articles of this kind fall within the scope of our business activities, we take this opportunity to express our wish to enter into business relations with you.

Chinese table-cloths are known for their good quality, attractive designs and fine workmanship. They have enjoyed great popularity in the European market. We believe that through our joint efforts they will also meet with a favorable reception in your country.

In our trade with merchants of various countries, we always adhere to the principle of equality and mutual benefit. The policy of ours greatly helps to strengthen trade relations and promote friendship between the Chinese people and the people of other countries. We are sure of good business prospects before us.

In order to give you a general idea of our table-cloths, we are sending you, under separate cover, a copy of the latest catalogue. If you find any of the items interesting, please let us know as soon as possible. We shall be glad to send you quotations and samples upon receipt of your detailed enquiry.

Your rapid specific enquiry will be appreciated.

Yours faithfully,

b. Reply

Dear Sirs,

We thank you for your letter dated March 3th, 2006, and shall be pleased to enter into trading relations with you.

After checking the catalogue, we are happy to inform you that we are interested in No.1314 and 1316 list in your catalogue. We shall be appreciative if you send us the samples of the two kinds, offer us the details of your prices and state the terms of payment.

In view of the demands for your products, an immediate reply is appreciated.

Yours faithfully,

2. General Enquiry and Reply

a. A General Enquiry

Dear Sir or Madam,

We have learned from the Commercial Counselor's Office of our Embassy in your country that you manufacture and export a variety of textile.

Our company is one of the importers of textile articles in London. As there is a steady demand for high quality cotton bed-sheets, we would like you to send us as soon as possible your illustrated catalogue, price-list and all necessary information about the goods.

We are large dealers in textiles and believe there is a promising market in our area for moderately priced goods mentioned above.

Your prompt attention will be much appreciated.

Yours faithfully,

b. Reply

Dear Sirs,

We are happy to receive your enquiry of May 26th, 2006, and enclose our illustrated catalogue and price-list you want. Also by separate post, we are sending you some samples, which will show you clearly the quality of our products.

If you purchase not less than 150 dozen of individual items we would grant you a discount of 3%. Payment is to be made by irrevocable and confirmed L/C.

Because of their softness and durability, all our cotton bed-sheets are very popular, and we often find difficulty in meeting the demand. But if you place an order not later than June 15th, 2006, we would ensure you a prompt shipment.

We call your attention to our other cotton products such as pillowcases, details of which you will find in the catalogue. Any orders may place with us will have our prompt attention.

Yours faithfully,

3. Specific Enquiry for Price and Reply

a. A Specific Enquiry for Price

Dear Sirs,

We are now in the market for large quantity of corn for the production of high quality wine and should be obliged if you would give us a quotation per metric ton CIF London, with the regular purchase of 5, 000 metric ton a year, and inform the earliest date you can ship.

We used to purchase corn from other sources, but we now prefer to buy from your corporation because we are given to understand you are able to supply larger quantities with a special discount. Besides, we are convinced that your corn is of better quality.

We look forward to hearing from you by return.

Yours faithfully,

b. Reply

Dear Sirs,

We thank you for your enquiry of June 18th, 2006. At your request, we are making you the following offer subject to your reply arriving here before July 10th.

"Not less than 5, 000 metric tons a year, at US$0.2 per metric ton CIF London for shipment within 2 weeks of receiving order, for payment by irrevocable L/C at sight. Please notice that the offer is subject to goods being unsold."

We hope that the above will be acceptable to you, and await with keen interest your formal orders.

Yours faithfully,

4. Specific Enquiry for Copy Machine and Reply

a. A Specific Enquiry for Copy Machine

Dear Mr. Li,

Nice to meet you during last Guangzhou Fair.

We are now interested in copy machine in bulk quantities, and shall be pleased if you send us ASAP your illustrated catalogues, latest price-list with quantities available and samples. And in your reply, please indicate the earliest date of shipment as well as your best quantity discount. Your rapid reply will be appreciated.

Yours faithfully,

b. Reply

Dear Mr. Robinson,

Thank you for your enquiry of May 10, 2006. Meanwhile, we enclose details of our copy machine for your examination.

All the models illustrated can be supplied from stock at competitive prices, shown on the price-list inside the catalogue. As we carry a large stock of the goods in superior quality, we can execute your commands promptly and faithfully, at the rock-bottom prices as shown in the price-list.

We guarantee shipment within 10 days after receipt of your order.

We are looking forward to your early order.

Yours sincerely,

Notes

1. enquiry n.询盘，询购，询价，同 inquiry。通常是指交易前，一方向另一方询问有关商品的价格、数量、交货时间、付款条件以及折扣等情况。多通过要求对方提供价目表、商品目录、样品、款式、型号等了解相关商品和市场
2. learn from… 收到……的来信，从……获知
3. fall within … 属于……，符合……
4. enter into… 开始(某种事业、对话、关系等)；缔结(契约、协议和合同)
5. take this opportunity to do… 借此机会做……，同 avail this opportunity of doing…
6. business relations 业务关系，商务关系，意思同 trade relations
7. workmanship n. 手艺，工艺，做工，技巧
8. adhere to… 坚持，追随
9.equality and mutual benefit 平等互利
10. give … a general idea of … 为了使……了解……
11. under separate cover 另函邮寄，在另函中。同 by separate post
12. catalogue n. (产品)目录
13. as soon as possible 尽快，常缩写为 ASAP
14. quotations n. 报价单，行情表，报价
15. upon/on receipt of… 一旦收到……就……
16. specific enquiry 具体询盘

17. appreciate　v. 涨价；感谢；理解
18. appreciative　adj. 表示感激的，承认有价值的
19. terms of payment　付款条件，付款方式
20. in view of…　鉴于，由于，考虑到
21. Commercial Counselor's Office　商务参赞处
22. illustrated catalogue　附有插图的目录
23. price-list　价目单，价格表
24. dealer　经销商
25. promising　有希望的，有前途的
26. enclose　v. 把……封入，把……附在信中，随函寄去……
27. discount　n. 折扣
28. irrevocable and confirmed L/C　不可撤销的保兑信用证
29. call one's attention to sth.　提请某人注意某事。类似的表达还有 invite one's attention to sth.；draw one's attention to sth.
30. in the market for…　想要购买……
31. CIF：Cost，Insurance and Freight 的缩写，译为"成本费，保险费，运费在内价"
32. be of…　具有……的性质，具有……的特征
33. at one's request　应某人的要求
34. offer　发盘，又称报盘、报价(详见第 3 单元)
35. subject to…　取决于……，决定于……
36. irrevocable L/C at sight　不可撤销的即期信用证
37. Chinese Export Commodities Fair，also called Canton Fair，or Guangzhou Fair　广交会。每年春秋两季各举行一次
38. for one's examination　供……参考，供……查阅。类似表达还有　for one's examination；for one's information；for one's reference；for one's study；for one's consideration

Exercises

I. Fill in the blanks with proper words or expressions and then translate the following into Chinese.

(1) We take ______ ______ ______ writing to you with a view to building up business relations with your corporation.

(2) Enclosed ______ ______ a copy of our price-list.

(3) We take the liberty ______ writing to you with a hope to get your best quantity discount for North-east rice.

(4) Your prompt ______ to this matter will be very much appreciated.

(5) We are indebted ______ Mr. Smith of AAA Co. for having recommended you ______ us as one of the leading importers in London.

(6) You are introduced to us by Robinson Co. ______ one of the leading dealers of hardware products.

(7) We have ______ your address ______ the Commercial Counselor's Office of your Embassy ______ Sydney.

(8) ______ receipt of your ______ enquiry, we shall airmail you immediately our quotation sheet.

(9) To give you a ______ idea of the ______ kinds of canned goods now ______ for export, we enclose a brochure.

(10) We are now in the ______ for enamelware of high quality.

(11) In compliance with your enquiry, we enclose the catalogue and price-list for your ______.

II. Fill in the blanks of the following letter.

Dear Sirs,

Through the ______ of our Commercial Counselor's Office in your country, we learned that you were one of the ______ importers of canned foodstuffs.

We like to take the ______ to introduce ourselves to you ______ a state-owned corporation ______ in exporting canned foodstuffs, and express our ______ to enter into business relations ______ you.

In order to give you some ______ of our exports, we are pleased to send you a copy of our ______ catalogue. Quotations and samples will be sent to you ______ receipt of your specific enquiries.

We expect hearing from you soon.

Yours faithfully,

III. Choose the appropriate words to fill in the blanks.

on; as; in; under; by; with; from; against; to; at

(1) Your firm has been kindly recommended to us by Messrs. J. Smith & Co. , Inc. ,in New

York, ______ large importers of office furniture.

(2) We are exporters of long standing and high reputation, engaged ______ exportation of following articles.

(3) Please let us know ______return what your experience has been in your dealings with them.

(4) If your price is competitive, we shall be glad to place a substantial order______ you.

(5) We have seen your advertisement ______ portable typewriters in "China Today".

(6) Some copies of our latest catalogues are being airmailed to you ______separate cover.

(7) We learned ______ ABC Co. that you are in a position to supply fruit and dried fruit.

(8) As for terms of payment, we need irrevocable L/C payable by draft ______sight.

(9) We used ______ import teacups from Korea, but now we divert our buying to your country.

(10) We enclose quotation sheet ______ your enquiry No.2233 and look forward to your confirmation.

IV. Translate the following into English.

(1) 承蒙我国驻纽约的大使馆介绍，得知贵公司专门经营棉质家居品的进口业务。我们愿意与贵公司建立业务关系。

(2) 我们对贵方在《今日中国》上所刊登的广告很感兴趣，请来函告知该商品的详细情况。

(3) 按照贵方要求，特随函附寄我们的附图产品目录，供你方参考。

(4) 一旦收到贵方的具体询盘，我们会立即给贵方寄送样品并报最优惠的价格。

(5) 我们是一家在全世界范围内经营进出口业务的贸易公司。

V. Translate the following into Chinese.

(1) We have received your enquiry of August 2 and learn of your interest in our Vacuum Cleaners MP208. We are now enclosing our illustrated catalogues and price list you asked for.

(2) We learn that you are very interested in China, so we take the liberty of writing to you.

(3) We are interested in various kinds of Chinese Arts and Crafts and should appreciate your catalogues and quotation.

(4) We are pleased to send you with this letter a copy of our current pricelist for candles in different colors and shapes.

(5) We have heard you are able to supply larger quantities at more competitive prices, so we prefer to buy from you.

VI. Writing.

Messrs. Arthur Grey & Son write to China National Import & Export Corporation, stating that they have an order to supply a hotel with table-cloths. They request samples in handsome designs of medium and best linen suitable for the purpose.

Supplementary Reading

Useful Sentences

(1) We regularly buy… and would like know what you have to offer.
我们定期购买……并且想知道贵公司的报价如何。

(2) We would like very much to continue to do business with you and are now awaiting your offer.我公司很乐意和你公司继续有业务往来，并正在等待你公司的报盘。

(3) As the brochures you sent us were badly damaged in the mail, we would like you to mail us some more.
贵公司寄来的产品简介小册子在邮寄途中已经完全损坏，希望你公司再多寄些来。

(4) Please tell us how long this price list is valid.
请告知我们这个价目单的有效期有多长。

(5) What quantities of the specified item can you regularly deliver on short notice?
请告知我们，短期内你公司能定期运送多少数量的上述产品？

(6) We would appreciate your sending us a catalogue of your …with terms of payment and the largest discount you can allow us.
请寄……目录，并注明你方要求的付款条件及能给予的最大折扣。

(7) Please send us your latest catalogue with your best CIF London prices. We will also appreciate your telling us the approximate weight of each article.
请寄附有最优惠的成本加保险费、运费到伦敦价的最新商品目录，并请告知每件货物的大约重量。

(8) We have the pleasure of sending you under separate cover, a new catalogue which lists the complete line of our ……goods. For your information, we checked the items which we hope especially interest you.
现另邮寄上我们全部……产品的新目录一本。为供你方参考，特标明那些我们认为你们会特别感兴趣的产品。

Unit 3 Quotations, Firm Offers & Counter Offers

Objective

Understanding and writing the letters connected with Quotations, Firm Offers &Counter Offers

Requirement

- Grasping the usual usage of professional words and sentences
- Grasping the professional terms of orders

Introduction

Quotations and offers are important steps of business negotiation. When a seller prepares to export, he quotes the potential buyer the price of the goods concerned on receipt of the enquiry.

A quotation is merely a notice of the price of certain goods at which the seller is willing to sell. People in China usually treat quotations as non-firm offers, which do not legally bind both parties. That is, the prospective buyer is under no obligation to buy the goods for which a quotation is requested, while the seller is not bound to sell what has been previously quoted. A price quotation with clear promise to sell can be considered an operative offer if it includes the essential terms of price and quantity and leaves settlements of this terms to a future agreement by the parties.

An offer refers to trading terms put forward by exporters to importers, on which the exporters are willing to conclude business with the importers. These terms mainly include name of commodity, brand, specifications, quantity, price, packing, payment and shipment, etc. Usually, there are two parties involved in an offer. The one who sends the offer is called the offeror and the one who receives the offer is the offeree.

There are two kinds of offers： non-firm offer and firm offer：

Non-firm offer, also means offer without engagement, is usually made by means of sending catalogues, price-lists, proforma invoice and quotations. Hereinto, quotations are seen most.

A firm offer is made when a seller promises to sell specific goods at a stated price and within a stated time. It must be communicated with the offeree and it must ensure that all essential terms are clearly definite. Once a firm offer has been accepted unconditionally within the term of validity it can not be withdrawn. When a firm offer is made, two major requirements must be concerned. First of all, the writer of a firm offer should enclose complete, affirmative, specific terms of business. That means, the major conditions of the contract are required as to time of delivery, shipping and terms of payment as well as names of goods, quality, specifications, prices, quantity, packing and insurance. Secondly, the validity period is indispensable to a firm offer. In other words, a firm offer will lose its binding force if it goes beyond the validity date.

A quotation or an offer may contain the following points：

(1) In the first part, you acknowledge the enquiry and thank for the buyer's interest in your products.

(2) In the middle part, you tell the situation of your stock and state all the terms and conditions in a complete, clear and definite way. In case of a firm offer, the validity must be exactly stated.

(3) In the last part, you should express your hope that the quotation or the offer will be to the correspondent's satisfaction and accepted.

Sometimes, with a view to expanding export trade, the sellers may make offers or quotations voluntarily according to the conditions, even though no enquiries are received from abroad. When the buyer initiates the offer to the seller, it is called a bid.

A counter-offer is an offer made in response to a previous offer by the other party during negotiations for a final contract. In other words, when a buyer rejects a quotation or other offer, or finds part of the offer unacceptable, he proposes amendments on the terms of the original offer and raises new ones in his counter offer. Making a counter-offer automatically rejects the prior offer. Usually, a counter-offer covers the following points:

(1) Thank the offeror for his offer.

(2) Express regret at inability to accept the offerors' offer.

(3) State reasons for non-acceptance.

(4) Make a counter-offer.

(5) Urge the offeree to accept the counter-offer.

Specimen letters

1. Quotation for Feige Brand Bicycle and the Buyer's Counter Offer

a. Quotation for Feige Brand Bicycle

Dear Sirs,

We thank you for your letter of 8th June, enquiring for Feige Brand bicycle.

We are exporting bicycles of various brands among which Feige and Forever brand are the most famous ones. They are in great demand abroad and our stocks are running down quickly. They are popular not only for their light weight, but also for the reasonable prices. We are confident that once you have tried our bikes you will place repeat orders with us in large quantities.

Based on your requirement, we are quoting as follows:

Feige Brand Bicycles:

20″	Men's Style	at US$20 per set
20″	Women's Style	at US$22 per set
26″	Men's Style	at US$22 per set
26″	Women's Style	at US$25 per set

Payment Terms: By L/C at sight to be opened through a bank to be approved by the sellers.

Shipment: September, 2006, provided the covering L/C reaches the sellers by the end of this year.

The above prices are understood to be on CIF New York basis. Please note that we do not allow any commission on our bicycles, but a discount of 3% may be allowed if the quantity for each specification is more than 1,000 sets.

The above quotation is made without engagement and is subject to our final confirmation.

Meanwhile, we would like to take this opportunity to introduce to you our Forever Brand bicycles which enjoy the same popularity as Feige Brand. Enclosed please find a copy of our illustrative catalogue which will give you all the details. We hope you will find them interesting and let us have your orders.

We look forward to your early reply.

Yours faithfully,

b. The Buyer's Counter Offer to the Above Letter

Dear Sirs,

We have received your letter of 18 June, 2006, quoting us Feige Brand bicycle. Thanks.

We have been very pleased with your product as you know. However, we would not accept your quotations unless you can grant us a discount of 5%.

In view of our long-standing business relationship, we make you such a counter, If you can see your way clear to meet these figures we would be pleased to place with you an order that will carry us for the rest of this year.

Please inform us of acceptance at your earliest convenience.

Yours faithfully,

2. Quotation for Leather Handbags and the Buyer's Counter Offer

a. Quotation for Leather handbags

Dear Sirs,

We thank you for your letter dated April 8 enquiring for leather handbags. As requested, we take pleasure in offering you, subject to our final confirmation, 500 dozens of deer skin handbags style No. MA 186 at $125.00 Per dozen CIF Hamburg. Shipment will be effected within 20 days after receipt of the relevant L/C issued by your first class bank in our favor upon signing Sales Contract.

We are manufacturing various kinds of leather purses and waistbelts for exportation, and under separate cover, a brochure of products has been sent to you by airmail today. We hope some of them would meet your customers' taste and need.

If we can be of any further help, please feel free to let us know. You may rest assured that any enquiry from you will meet with our careful attention.

Yours faithfully,

b. The Buyer's Counter Offer

Dear Sirs,

We acknowledge the receipt of both your offer of June 3rd and the brochure of your leather purses and waistbelts, thank you for these.

While appreciating the good quality of your products, we find your price is too high for the market we wish to supply.

We also have to point out that the leather handbags are available on our market from several North America manufacturers, all of them are at prices from 15%to 20% below yours.

Such being the case, we have to ask you to consider if you can make reduction in your price, say 15%. As our order would be worth around Stg. 50,000, you may think it worthwhile to make a concession.

We await with keen interest your rapid reply.

Yours faithfully,

3. A Firm offer for Shoes by the Seller

Dear Sirs,

Thank you for your enquiry of March 6 regarding our Man's Casual Shoes. Considering our long business relations, we would like to make you special offer as follows:

Commodity：Hiking Brand Man's Casual Shoes

Specifications：Brown Rubber Soles, Black Cotton Uppers

Sizes：Large 45%, Medium 55%

Packing：Each pair in a poly bag, two dozens to an enforced carton

Quantity：100dozen

Price：US$4, 500 each dozen CIF New York

Shipment：April/May 2006

Payment：By Confirmed Irrevocable L/C Payable at sight

This is our firm offer, subject to your immediate acceptance.

We await your reply in cable.

Yours faithfully,

4. A Firm Offer for Raincoat

Dear Sirs,

Thank you for your enquiry of March 22, and we take pleasure in quoting the price as shown in the following firm offer delivered today subject to acceptance by 5p.m. on April 5th.

Please note this offer is firm. We are unable to entertain any counter offer. We quote as follows：

Commodity： Rainbow raincoat

Quantity and price：

50 men's large-sized coats	$12.20 each	$610.00
100 men's medium-sized coats	$11.20 each	$1, 120.00
100 men's small-sized coats	$10.20 each	$1, 020.00
100 women's medium-sized coats	$11.50 each	$1, 150.00
100women's small-sized coats	$10.50 each	$1, 050.00
Total price		$4, 950.00
Less 11% trade discount		$544.50
Net price		$4, 405.50

Shipment：within 2weeks after receiving order

With the approach of the rain season, there has been an increasing demand for high quality raincoats. As regards "Rainbow" rainwear, it is not only lightweight but creaseless on its inside surface because of special treatment. "Rainbow" raincoats are made from very best quality material and can be supplied in a range of designs and colors wide enough to meet the requirements of a fashionable trade such as yours.

We trust you will take advantage of this seasonal opportunity and favor us with an early reply.

Yours faithfully,

5. the Sellers' Counter Offer

Dear Sirs,

In reply to your letter of June 8 requesting a 7% allowance, we regret we find it very difficult to comply with.

You say you can get shoes of the same quality at much lower prices, but we are sure that our products are far superior in quality to any other shoes of the same price level. In actuality, the prices we quoted are closely calculated. Thanks to the high quality, considerable business has been done with many customers in other markets at these prices. You will be convinced of the reasonableness of our offer through a fair comparison of quality between our products and similar products from other sources. Therefore, considering the quality of the goods offered we do not feel that the prices we quoted are at all excessive, but bearing in mind the special character of your trade and the good and longstanding business relations between us, we have decided to offer you a special discount of 3% on an order amounting to $10,000 or over.

If you find our proposal acceptable, please let us have your order at an early date. We assure you that we always do our utmost to execute your order to your complete satisfaction.

Yours faithfully,

Notes

1. offer　n. 发盘，又称报盘、报价。报盘是对询盘的回复，是卖方按其所述条款供应货物。在报盘中，卖方不仅报他想要销售的货物的价格，还要报出其他交易条款，如付款条件、交货日期等，以供买方考虑。通常和介词 for、of 或 on 连用
2. Firm offer　实盘。发盘人有肯定的订立合同的旨意，一旦发盘人在有效期内表示完全同意，交易即达成
3. Non-firm offer　虚盘。发盘人没有肯定的订立合同的旨意，如发盘内容不明确、发盘主要内容不完备、发盘不是最终的等，这种发盘对发盘人无约束力
4. bid　vt. 出价，投标；n. 出价，投标；v. 支付
5. quotation　报价(只涉及价格)
6. counter offer　还盘，还价。交易的一方在接到一项发盘后，不能完全同意而针对该发盘内容(如价格、支付方式、转运期、付款方式等)提出修改建议
7. provided　只要，以…为条件
8. covering　附加说明的，前面提到的
9. in one's favor　有利于某人，对某人有利，(信用证等)以某人为受益人，(开)给某人

10. effect v. 实现，完成(装运，投保等)
11. Stg. sterling 的缩写。n. 英国货币(尤指英国基本货币单位英镑), 标准纯银
12. make a concession 作出让步

Exercises

I. Fill in the blanks with proper words or expressions and then translate the following into Chinese.

(1) Please send us a ______ for the supply of 25 ton No.45 chemical fertilizer.

(2) With ______ ______ your enquiry of July 8th, we shall be pleased to supply 50 sets of copy machine at the price of $200 each.

(3) We take the ______ to enclose herewith ______ your reference the newest samples and our revised catalogue and price list. This cancels the previous lists.

(4) The quotation we offer you at exceptionally low prices are ______ ______ reply by return of post.

(5) As the market is ______ your price is ______ on the high side.

(6) We cannot ______ ______ ______ clear to reduce the price to the level you ______.

(7) We learn from your letter of June 8th that our price for the subject article is found to be ______ the ______ ______.

(8) ______ request, we take pleasure ______ sending you herewith a copy of our illustrated catalogue.

(9) We have cut our price to the limit. We regret, therefore, being unable to comply ______ your request for further reduction.

(10) Since considerable business has been done ______ this price, we trust that it will also be acceptable ______ you.

II. Fill in the blanks of the following letter.

Dear Sirs,

In ______ with your request of June 10th, we are ______ to send you, under separate cover, a copy of our catalogue together ______ the revised price-list, showing the ______ price of our supplies.

The catalogue ______ illustration and descriptions of the large varieties of cameras made ______ Japan. We ask you to compare our prices ______ those of other company. We are confident that you will appreciate the special value we offer you.

We should esteem and give very careful ______ to any orders received from you.

Yours faithfully,

III. Choose the appropriate words to fill in the blanks.

line; offer; reduction; quote; by return; discontinue; covering; decline; withdrawn; increasing

(1) Unless you see your way clear to grant us an additional reduction in price, we may have to ______ our business with you.

(2) It is regrettable that we have to ______ your counter offer.

(3) In reply to your letter of quotation, we regret very much to say that our customers here find your price rather on high side and out of ______ with the prevailing market level.

(4) As you see, the market is firm with an upward tendency. Such being the case, there is much likelihood of price ______ in the near future.

(5) Considering our long-standing friendly business relationship, we can allow you ______ of 4% in our price.

(6) Please ______ us your lowest prices for both men's and women's winter jackets.

(7) Please ______ us 500 glass vases CIF Dalian, China.

(8) Enclosed please find our quotation sheet ______ different sizes and colors of our banners.

(9) The offer is to be ______ if not accepted by the end of this month.

(10) Please let us know ______ the lowest prices at which you can execute this order, CIF Boston.

IV. Translate the following into English.

(1) 我们确认已向贵方电报下列商品实盘，以 9 月 20 日前回复有效。

(2) 获悉你地市场对核桃有很大需求，兹附上第 6868 号报价单供参考。

(3) 你方 6 月 3 日来电要求我们报第 33 号毯子。现确认我方于 6 月 6 日电报向你方报盘如下，该盘不受约束。

(4) 贵方 7 月 9 日来函收悉，谢谢。很遗憾，贵方价格偏高，无法成交。

(5) 感谢贵方 7 月 10 日的询问，我方很高兴以每台 110 美元的报价供应 50 台扫描仪。

(6) 获悉贵方认为我们降价之后的报价仍然太高，我们感到很遗憾。无论如何，在不牺牲产品质量的条件下，我们尽了最大努力，以尽可能低的价格向贵公司报价。

V. Translate the following into Chinese.

(1) We are sorry that we are unable to entertain any counter offer, for this offer is firm, subject to the receipt of reply by us before May 8th.

(2) With regard to the minimum quantity of 10,000 yards per design which you asked for in your cable, we have to point out that in your previous letter of 20th March the minimum was 8500 yards.

(3) The respective quantities are quoted on the basis of CFR Port Copenhagen. This offer is subject to our final confirmation. As to the relative samples, we have dispatched them to you by separate airmail.

(4) We must stress that this offer is firm for 5days only because of the heavy demand for the limited supplies of this velvet in stock.

(5) Confirming our telephone conversation this morning, we can offer you the rice of 400 lbs, at the special price of $80 per lb., CIF London.

(6) The Chinese velvet curtains are of good quality and have fine workmanship and look good. They are moderately priced, which is known to all.

VI. Writing.

Write a letter for a curtain material manufacturer, with a quotation enclosed therein, giving favorable comments on the goods offered and recommending their client's acceptance.

Supplementary Reading

Useful Sentences

(1) We offer you firm subject to reply by 5 p.m. our time, Monday, July 10.
兹报实盘，以我方时间 7 月 10 日星期一下午 5 时以前答复为有效。

(2) We offer you firm subject to reply here by 11 a.m., Tuesday our time.
兹报实盘，以我方时间星期二上午 11 时以前回复为准。

(3) We offer you firm subject to your reply here within one week from today.
兹报实盘，以自本日起一周之内你方回复为准。

(4) We are ready to sell …
我方准备卖……商品。

(5) We offer … subject to our final confirmation.

我方报盘……(各项交易条件)……以我方最后确认为准。

(6) We make you an offer subject to the goods being unsold.

我方向你方报盘，以未售出为准。

(7) We submit you this offer subject to prior sale.

我方向你方报盘，以先售为条件。

(8) We offer you subject to change without notice.

我方向你方报盘，此报盘如有变化不另行通知。

(9) This offer must be withdraw if not accepted within 5 days.

此盘五日内不接受，就作撤销论。

(10) We will keep this offer open up to the end of this month.

我方保留该报盘至本月底。

(11) If you can raise your order to 1, 000 dozen，we can offer you a price of CIF U.S.$30 per each.

倘若贵公司能提高订购的数量到 1000 打，我公司就能提供每样 CIF30 美元的价格。

(12) Unfortunately, we cannot accept your offer. Your prices are prohibitive.

遗憾，我们不能接受你方报盘，你方价格过高，不敢问津。

(13) Your offer dated … is very attractive. However, the quantity offered is too small to satisfy our requirements. Would you be able to process a big order for a quality of … item No. …?

贵公司…月…日所寄来的报价单甚具吸引力，然而，供应量太少，无法满足我们的需要量。不知贵公司能否生产品目第……号，数量……的较大订单。

Unit 4 Orders & Acknowledgements

Objective

- Understanding and writing the letters connected with orders and acknowledgement
- Reading and understanding the relative documents

Requirement

- Knowing what are mainly included in order letters and how to confirm them
- Grasping the usual usage of professional expressions and sentences
- Grasping the professional terms of orders

Introduction

What is an order? When you go to a shop, you ask the tailor or dressmaker to make you a coat or a dress according to your measurement. That's an order.

It is rather complicated in international trade. Going through enquiry and quotation and many a round of offer and counter offer, both parties come to an agreement and the buyer places an order with the seller. Up to then, business reaches the most important stage. An order is a written notification of purchase from buyers to sellers, demanding sellers to supply the goods or services in accordance with the order. Nowadays, many big companies use official printed order forms, which save time and ensure that no information be ignored. Still there are companies, small companies particular, who place orders in the form of letters. An order becomes legally binding upon either party after confirmation and later serves as the basis to open a credit letter on. Accuracy is essential in the placing of an order, for any error can bring about unexpected trouble which is irrecoverable later. See to it that the language used in an order letter is definite, exact and simple.

Seller should acknowledge the receipt of order in written form without delay, no matter he or she accepts or rejects them.

Specimen Letters

1. Order of Pillowcases and the Seller's Acknowledgement

a. Order of Pillowcases

Dear Sirs,

<u>Our Order No.1</u>

Please forward the following merchandise to us：

Quantity	Pattern No	Catalogue No	Prices
800 pillowcases	16	31	US$1.65 each
700 pillowcases	21	37	US$1.75 each

(All the prices are FOB Shanghai)

Delivery：During September

Payment：By L/C to be opened in accordance with our agreement

Packing: Usually packing in strong bales, with gunny bag cover and waterproof material.

Please acknowledge this order immediately on receipt and inform definite delivery date. This order is of no avail if it is not signed by a responsible person of our firm.

Faithfully yours,

(signature)

Mark Smith

b. the Seller's Acknowledgement

Dear Sirs,

Thank you for your Order No.1 for pillowcases and assure you that all the items you required are in stock. We are happy that you become one member of our customers.

We confirm with you the following order for the pillowcases at the prices stated in your letter of March 2nd, 2007:

Our Order No.1

Quantity	Pattern No	Catalogue No	Prices
800 pillowcases	16	31	US$1.65 each
700 pillowcases	21	37	US$1.75 each

(All the prices are FOB Shanghai)

Delivery: During September

Payment: By L/C to be opened in accordance with our agreement

Packing: Usually packing in strong bales, with gunny bag cover and waterproof material.

For the above order, we enclose our Purchase Confirmation No.216 in duplicate. Please sign and return one copy for our file at your earliest convenience.

We are expected to arrange the establishment of the relative Confirmed Irrevocable Letter of Credit through the bankers and you should inform us by fax as soon as it is opened.

We thank you again for the above order and hope that this will lead to an enduring cooperation between us.

Yours truly,

2. Order of Tea and the Sellers' Acceptance

a. Placing An Order of Tea

Dear Sirs,

Thank you for your speedy samples, along with the quotation for your tea of October 5th.

We have made selections from the samples you sent on October 30th. We found the quality of the tea meets our requirement and we take pleasure of placing you the order as follows, which we commend to your immediate and best attention:

200 kilograms Xihu Dragon Well tea

300 kilograms Shifeng Dragon Well tea

As it is the first time for your goods to be introduced here, we think the relative literatures may help promote the sales. Hope you will send us them at your earliest convenience.

We shall be appreciated if you kindly let us have the shipping advice immediately after you effect shipment.

Our order is subject to your acceptance of our usual terms of payment, viz.30 days after sight. If this first order proves satisfactory, we shall be happy to place further orders with you.

Yours faithfully,

b. the Seller's Acceptance

We thank you very much for your kind order for our tea which we have received. It has our immediate and careful attention.

You may rest assured that the tea under the order has been carefully packaged in chest to prevent damage in transit. We shall send you the shipping advice and the invoice at the time of shipment by this May.

The terms of payment you suggested are acceptable, and you may rely on us to give all your orders prompt attention.

Since it is the best season for tea, we hope you make full use of the opportunity. I am sure you will be pleased to collect good comments on our tea from your consumers, and build up a market for the product in your country.

We hope this will lead to more considerable orders.

Yours faithfully,

3. the Sellers' Rejecting

Dear Sirs,

<u>Order No.123</u>

It is appreciated that you handed us your order No.123 for 2,500 women's shirts.

However, we are sorry that we are fully committed with contract orders because the sales season for women's shirts is coming. As it is the case, we have no other alternative but to decline your order of this time. But we assure you that your future favors and orders will have our immediate attention.

We are always at your service.

Yours faithfully,

4. the Seller Offering Substitute

Dear Sirs,

Thank you for your letter dated March 15th, 2005, ordering 10, 000 pieces of Rainbow Raincoat Mode 2.

We regret that we can no longer supply the said raincoats, which are out of production. In their place we would like to offer our Rainbow Raincoat Mode 3. This is our new design, made of light, durable and waterproof material. The quality of this article is excellent, but the price is 5% lower. The large number of repeat orders we regularly receive from leading distributions is a clear evidence of the widespread popularity of Rainbow Raincoat Mode 3.

Full details of our export prices and terms of business are enclosed with this letter. Our illustrated catalogues and sales literature are being sent by separate cover.

You can be sure of our immediate attention to your order, which we are looking forward to receiving.

Yours faithfully,

Relative Documents

1. Sales Contract

Sellers:　　　　Contract No：2006GR-6320

Date：Dec 5th, 2006

For account of：________________

Buyers:　　　　Telex/fax：____________

This Contract is signed by and between the Buyers and the Sellers, Whereby the Buyers agree to buy and the Sellers agree to sell the under-mentioned commodity according to the terms and conditions stipulated below:

(1) Name of commodity and specifications, quantity, unit price and total value：

Name of Commodity and Specifications	Quantity	Unit Price	Amount
FUSED SILICA GRADE 1			CFR MOJI
Lot No.：031103			
Specification：		USD504/MT	USD20,160
SiO_2 99.99% min			
Al_2O_3 300ppm max			
Fe_2O_3 50ppm max			
Na_20 40ppm max			
K_2O 0.5ppb max	Shipment 5% more or less at seller's option		
Size：0.5-10mm 90% min			

(2) Total Value of Contract：

Say U.S. Dollars

(3) Packing：

In 1MT big bag with two layers and bottom discharging spout and then 2 big bags on one pallet

(4) Shipping Mark：

FUSED SILICA (LU)

GR-MW

LOT NO：031103

(5) Port of shipment：JIUJIANG, P.R. CHINA

(6) Port of destination：MOJI, JAPAN

(7) Time of shipment：In the middle of Dec.2006

(8) Insurance：TO BE COVERED BY SELLERS

(9) Terms of payment：

CFR Terms

① The carrying vessel shall be provided by the sellers, with partial shipment and transshipment allowed.

② After loading is completed, the Seller shall advise the Buyers by telex or fax of the contract number, name of commodity, quantity, name of the carrying vessel and date of shipment.

(10) Claims: In case of quality discrepancy and /or quantity discrepancy. Claims shall be lodged by the Buyers within 15 days after arrival of the goods at the port of destination. It is understood that Sellers shall not be reliable for any discrepancy of the goods shipped due to causes for which the Insurance Company, Shipping Company, and other transportation organization /or Post Office are reliable.

(11) Force Majeure: The Sellers shall not be held responsible if they, owing to Force Majeure cause of causes, fail to make delivery within the time stipulated in the Contract or cannot deliver the goods, however, in such a case, the Sellers shall inform the Buyers immediately by telex or fax and, if it is requested by the Buyers, shall also deliver to the Buyers by registered post a certificate attesting the existence of such a cause or causes.

(12) Arbitration: Any dispute arising from the execution of, or in connection with, this Contract should be settled through negotiation. In case no settlement can be reached, the case shall then be submitted to China International Economic and Trade Arbitration Commission Beijing, for settlement by arbitration in accordance with the Commission's Provisional Rules of Procedure. The award rendered by the Commission shall be final and binding on both Parties.

(13) Effectiveness of the contract: This contract shall include two pages and come into force after the authorized signature by the Buyers and Sellers on the second page.

Sellers   Buyers

2. Purchase Order

Jinzhou Cereals, Oils & Foodstuffs Imp.&Exp. Corp.

169, Shiying Rd. Jinzhou 121000, CHINA

Tel.: (86)41699945678   Fax: (86)41699945678

PURCHASE ORDER No.111

We confirm our agreement on purchase of the following goods:

Description: A1 Grade Canned Mushroom of the following six qualities:

A.6×68 oz. Stem & Piece   B.24×16 oz. Button Slice

C.42×16 oz Whole Slice　　D.24×8 oz Button

E.48×4 oz. Whole　　F. 48×4 oz. Stem & Piece

Quantity：(Case)

A.1, 500　　B. 1, 000

C.2, 500　　D. 2, 000

E.1, 000　　F. 1, 200

Packing：By standard export case of 120 cans each.

Unit Price：CIF net New York per case in U.S. dollars

A.12.80　　B. 13.50

C.13.40　　D. 12.90

E.12.80　　F. 11.20

Payment：100% by irrevocable letter of credit opened immediately through First National City Bank, N.Y. and drawn at sight.

Delivery：For Items A to D：Prompt shipment

For Items E and F：One month after receipt of L/C

Shipping Marks：On each and every case, the following shipping mark should be stenciled.

SEATTLE

No.1—UP

Remarks：

① Sample cans of each quality to be air-freighted to us for approval.

② In addition to the ordinary shipping documents, please also submit a Certificate of Origin for each shipment.

Notes

1. order　n. 订单

place an order with…　向……下订单

place a regular order with…　与……定期订购

repeat order　续订单，重复订货

trial order　试订单

2. acknowledgement n. 回执；回信；承认，确认
3. merchandise n. 商品
4. pillowcase n. 枕套
5. bale n. 大包
6. gunny adj. 粗麻布的
   gunny bag 麻袋
7. waterproof adj. 防水的
8. responsible adj. 负责的
   responsible person 负责人
9. in stock 有现货
10. purchase confirmation 购买确认书
11. speedy adj. 迅速的，快速的
12. selection n. 挑选，选择，精选
13. as follows 如下，下列
14. sales literature (没有复数形式)文字说明；商业文字宣传品的总称
15.sales 销售量；销售额；销售的
   sales season 销售旺季
16. 30 days after sight 见票 30 天付款
17. attention n. 注意；从事；处理
18. You may rest assured that… 请放心……
19. prevent vt. 防止，阻止
20. transit vt. 运送，运输，运转
21. acceptable adj. 合意的，可接受的，受欢迎的
22. rely on 依赖，依靠
23. comment n. 评论，评语
24. consumer n. 消费者
25.build up n. 变得更大/更多/更强
26. substitute n. 替代品
27. supply vt. 供应，提供；满足需求

28. the said raincoat 上述商品(雨衣)

29. in place of 替代

30. be made of 由……构成

31. illustrated catalogues 附有插图的目录

Exercises

I. Choose the best answer to complete each of the following sentences.

(1) We confirm exchange of letters______the subject article.

A. to regard B. regarded C. regarding

(2) We are pleased to______business only on these terms.

A. transact B. transaction C. transacting

(3) ______is our Sales Confirmation in duplicate, a copy of which please sign and return to us for our file.

A. Enclose B. Enclosed C. Enclosing

(4) We look forward to______your further order.

A. receiving B. receive C. hearing from

(5) We believe such an arrangement will prove______.

A. satisfaction B. satisfactory C. satisfied

(6) We hope the goods will give you every ______.

A. satisfying B. satisfactory C. satisfaction

(7) Your offer is not______to us.

A. interested B. interest C. interesting

(8) The quality of the goods does not______us.

A. interest B. interesting C. interested

(9) Much to our______, we can not at present take any fresh orders for our shoes.

A. regretting B. regrettable C. regret

(10) As soon as we are______a position to accept new orders, we will contact you immediately.

A. at B. on C. in

II. Choose the appropriate words to fill in the blanks.

prices; of; stock; place; against; acceptable; with

Dear Sirs,

Thank you for your letter______April 12th sending us patterns of cotton prints. We find both quality and______satisfactory and are pleased to give you an order for some items on the standing that they will be supplied from current______at the prices named.

We expect to find a good market for these cottons and hope to______further and larger orders ______you in the near future.

Our usual terms of payment are cash______documents and we hope they will be______to you.

Please send us your confirmation of sales in duplicate.

Sincerely,

III. Translate the following into Chinese.

(1) We await the favor of your commands which shall have our prompt attention.

(2) We are willing to purchase 50 cases of china tea sets, provided that you sell them at a price not exceeding RMB 100.00 per set.

(3) Please give this order your best attention, and send them by express.

(4) We are arranging for dispatch next month.

(5) As our customers are badly in need of these goods, we hope you will send them at an early date.

IV. Translate the following into English.

(1) 你方报价不切实际，我客户难以接受，他们已向他处订货。

(2) 由于原材料缺乏，制造厂被迫停止接受新的订单。

(3) 我们要说明一下，由于大量需求，我们只能接受 8 月船期的订单。

(4) 如能收到贵方订单，我们将非常感谢。

(5) 我们非常高兴向贵公司订购下列商品。

(6) 请按照贵公司提供的样品给我们寄送 600 条床单。

(7) 贵方任何时候的订货都将得到我们全力而迅速的办理。

(8) 如果贵公司惠赐订单，我们将竭尽全力，保证令你方满意。

V. Translate the following letter into English.

尊敬的大卫先生：

您好！兹收到你方第 4845 号销售合同一式两份，按照你方要求，我们已经会签，随函退回一份。

有关信用证已通过中国银行纽约分行开出。收到后请立即安排装运，并电告船名和开航日期。

王伟　谨上

2007 年 3 月 21 日

VI. Writing

Write a letter with the following given particulars.

(1) 确认收到卖方寄来的样品，表示感谢。

(2) 订购 300 件女士羊毛衫，大中小号各 100 件。

(3) 要求迅速发货。

(4) 随函附上汇票一份以支付货款。

Unit 5 Packing

Objective

- Understanding and writing the letters connected with packing
- Reading and understanding the relative documents

Requirement

- knowing why to pack goods and what specific terms and conditions should be included in packing
- knowing the essential components of a letter which concerns packing
- mastering typical sentences and expressions in writing such letters

Introduction

Packing is one of the main business conditions to negotiate in the international business activities. It is considered as an important part of export business. Packing is of more and more competitive significance in international trade. Accordingly, the significance of packing has been increasingly recognized. It is absolutely necessary sometimes for a buyer to inform a seller in writing of specific packing terms or to have negotiations between the two sides on packing terms.

Products have to be packed before they are transported by any conveyance, so it is thought that packing is part of the product. Packing refers to the general operation of putting the goods into containers for shipment and storage, while packaging is how to pack goods with specialized containers and wrapping materials. There are two types of packing. They are：

(1) Transportation packing or outer packing.

(2) Packing for sale or inner packing.

The purpose of outer packing is to protect goods from damaging or stealing, facilitate transporting, loading, unloading and carrying, and economize freight cost, lower possible customs duties and insurance premium, create convenience for storage and check. Outer packing uses cases, bales, barrels, bags, baskets, pallets or containers to pack goods. In outer packing, such stuffing materials as paper scrap, paper wool, wood shavings, saw dust, waterproof paper and different plastics are necessary for prevention of shaking, breakage, dampness and rust. Inner packing is not only designed to protect goods, but also to help customers identify goods, make goods appeal to customers, beautify the look of goods, increase the sales, publicize the goods, help to display and sell goods, make goods easy to carry and use.

Specimen Letters

1. the Buyer Agrees to the Packing

Dear Sirs,

Order No.1234 Camera

We have received your favor of January 20th, and thank you very much for informing us that the subject goods are packed in cartons as usual practice.

We agree that you pack the above order in cartons, since you told us you have been using cartons of cameras for so many years and that any damage due to the packing has never occurred on the way of transportation. As you stated, packing the cameras in cartons will prevent skillful pilferage; such cartons are well protected against moisture; they are light and convenient to handle, etc. After study and investigation, we find that your comments sound quite reasonable.

In addition, we would hope the inner packing could be much attractive, and the design of the patterns and color could suit the taste of the young.

Hopefully the result of packing in cartons turns out to our satisfaction. If so, you may continue using this packing in the future. And we are looking forward to your shipment advice.

Yours faithfully,

2. Proposal of Container

Dear Sirs,

Re: Packing of Order No. 12

We refer to our order No.12 for TV sets, which you are going to use cardboard boxes to pack.

We are afraid that the cardboard boxes are not strong enough for transport by sea, so we propose that the consignment be sent by container service. What's more, soft packing stuffing material should be used all round the machines, but not just under and over. This kind of packing does not cost more, and it can effectively protect the goods from being damaged by rough handling. We believe these precautions are necessarily taken into account.

Hope to receive your letter of confirmation soon.

Yours faithfully,

3. A Reply of Packing

Dear Sirs,

Re: Packing for Shengli Men's Pants

In conformity with the request made in your letter of August 19th, we have much pleasure in explaining the reason why we use cartons for packing as well as describing how we pack the goods in accordance with the packing terms given in the contract.

We pack the goods in cartons of 4 dozen each. The inner packing is beautifully designed gift box, and you will find them ideal for gift presenting and surely a help for sale.

As for the outer packing, we prefer cartons, for packing in cartons has numerous advantages. First, it prevents skillful pilferage. The traces of pilferage will be more evident so that they are pretty helpful for the underwriter to compensate for such losses. Second, cartons are quite suitable for transport by sea. Packing in cartons has become popular in international shipment and insurance companies are ready to accept it for WPA and TPND. Third, the cartons have plastic lining that keeps the contents from dampness. One more reason is that cartons are more convenient to handle in the course of loading and unloading as they are comparatively light and impact. The last but not the least reason is that the freight charge may not be very expensive since the kind of container is light.

We hope the above comment will serve your purpose and look forward to your early reply.

Yours sincerely,

4. Acknowledgement of Packing

Dear Sirs,

We have received your letter of February 3rd concerning the packing details. We are pleased to acknowledge them as follows:

The rice under the Order No.454 should be packed in international standard rice sacks, gross weight about 50 kilos a sack, 500 sacks in an FCL container.

The packing described about is seaworthy export packing and fits for long distance ocean transportation.

On the outer packing please mark the original place, the port of destination and the order number. For the sake of precaution, warning mark like KEEP DRY should be shown, too.

We state the above for your information and shall fulfill your order accordingly if we do not hear from you to the contrary before the end of this month.

Yours faithfully,

PEARD &Co.

(signature)

Mark

Relative Document

Packing list

Xincheng RESOURCES CO., LTD.

Rm 1810, Green Field Building

No.233, Jianguo Road, Linghe District,
Dalian 116000 China

PACKING LIST

Contract No.: 2007GR-2021 Date: April 4th, 2007

Invoice No.: GR20072021

Marks & Nos	Commodity	Quantity	Weight

GRAPHITE FLAKE PLUS 195-20MT
20 BAGS /20MT
GRAPHITE
FLAKE
PLUS195 N.W.: 20,000kgs
MCL G.W.: 20,200kgs
GRAPHITE KLAKE PLUS 197-20MT
20BAGS/20MT
GRAPHITE
FLAKE
PLUS197 N.W.: 20,000kgs
MCL G.W.: 20,200kgs

PACKING: PACKED IN 40×25KG CRAFT PAPER BAGS AND THEN IN 1MT BIG BAGS.

NOTATIONS:

GOODS SHIPPED AS PER BUYER'S PURCHASE ORDER NO.PM/M/48/03-04/00250 DATED 21.02.2007

TOTAL: 40MTS/40BAGS
N.W.: 40,000KGS
G.W.: 40,400KGS

Vessel Name：OOCL FIDELITY B.0865
B/L NO.：ATSN601639
B/L Date：APR.15, 2007
L/C NO.：0750204DC000192

Notes

1. pack v. 包装
   repack v. 重新包装
   packing n. 包装
   package n. 包件
   outer packing 外包装
   inner packing 内包装
   neutral packing 中性包装
   packing list 装箱单
2. favor n./v. 恩惠；书信(=your letter)；喜爱；赞成；支持
   in favor of =in one’s favor 以……为受益人
3. subject adj./n. 标题的；主题；事由
4. due to 由于，因为
5. occur vi. 发生
6. protect vt. 保护；警戒
7. convenient adj. 方便的，便利的
8. handle vt. 装卸；经营；处理
   handle roughly 野蛮装卸
   handle with care 小心轻放
9. turn out (后接不定式)结果是，证明是
10. refer to 使某人参阅、关于、询问；谈到；涉及
11. propose v. 提出，提议
12. consignment n. 托运；发运；货物
13. stuffing n. 填充物，填料
14. precaution n. 预防措施
15. in conformity with… 与……相一致，依照……

16. as well as…　和；也
17. design　v. 设计；设计图，图案
18. ideal　adj. 理想的，完美的，不切实际的
19. present　adj. 赠送；呈递
20. as for　adj. 关于，至于
21. numerous　adj. 很多的；无数的
22. serve　adj. 用做，适合，为……尽职责
23. concerning　prep. 关于，有关
24. gross　adj. 总的；毛重的
    gross weight　毛重
    gross domestic product (GDP)　国内生产总值
25. seaworthy　adj. 适合航海的，经得住航海的
26. mark　v. 做标志于　n. 记号，标志
    shipping mark　运输标志，唛头
27. destination　n. 目的地
    destination port　目的港
28. for the sake of　为了……的好处；因……的缘故
29. fulfill　vt. 完成；履行；实现
30. contrary　adj. 相反的；adv. 相反地
    on the contrary　相反地

Exercises

I. Choose the best answer to complete each of the following sentences.

(1) We are satisfied the packing is suitable for a long sea _______.

A. trip　　B. voyage　　C. journey

(2) Please be _______ that your comments on packing will be passed on to our manufacturers for their reference.

A. sure　　B. ensure　　C. assured

(3) We are confident that our cartons for canned goods are not only _______ but also strong enough to protect the goods from any possible damage.

A. seaworthy　　B. seaworth　　C. for sea

(4) We shall ______ the 50 books to a carton.

A. put　　B. place　　C. pack

(5) Claims ______ transportation should be referred to the shipping company.

A. concerned　　B. concerning　　C. concern

(6) Almost two weeks have passed______ we emailed you our offer on September 30.

A. since　　B. when　　C. as

(7) ______ that it is necessary to protect the goods from any conceivable losses, you should insure them against all possible risks.

A. Consider　　B. Considering　　C. To consider

(8) ______ instructions are stated accurately in the captioned contract.

A. Packing　　B. Package　　C. Pack

(9) All the goods are to be ______ in wooden cases.

A. packing　　B. packed　　C. pack

(10) The ______ are intact.

A. pack　　B. package　　C. packs

II. Choose the appropriate words to fill in the blanks.

Inform;　be;　received;　to;　each;　met;　damage;　avoid

Dear Sirs,

Today we ______ your consignment of 40 cardboard cartons of safety pins. We regret to ______ you that 20 cartons were delivered damaged and the contents had spilled, leading______ some losses.

We accept that the ______ was not your fault but feel that we must modify our packing requirements to______future losses. We require that future packing ______ in wooden boxes of 25 kilos net, ______ wooden box containing 40 cardboard packs of 500 grams net.

Please let us know whether these specifications can be ______ by you and whether they will lead to an increase in your prices.

Yours sincerely,

III. Translate the following into Chinese.

(1) Mark the cases with the wording "FRAGILE" and "HANDLE WITH CARE", and number consecutively.

(2) We are afraid that we shall have to charge more for the designated packing, as it calls for extra labor and cost.

(3) To our surprise, the cases are intact but the contents are short.

(4) A well-designed, beautifully-decorated package helps sell the goods.

(5) The sun-flower oil is supplied in tins of 10 kilograms net, four tins to a crate.

(6) Tea must be packed in wooden cases lined with water proof material.

(7) The packing must be in line with local consumers' preference.

(8) It is necessary to take precautions to protect the goods from moisture.

(9) Owing to faulty packing, several of them arrived in such a bad condition that we were compelled to dispose of them at greatly reduced prices.

(10) Fountain pens are packed 10 pieces to a box and 300 boxes to a wooden case.

IV. Translate the following into English.

(1) 一切货物均须用内衬为锡纸的木箱包装，且外壳必须清楚地标明其内所装物品。

(2) 根据合同规定，唛头由买方选定。

(3) 我们保证包装很结实，能够经得住野蛮搬运。

(4) 花生用袋子装，每袋装 50 千克。

(5) 只要包装适于海运，我们不介意货物是用纸箱还是木箱包装。

(6) 我方建议这批货物改用中性包装，希望同意。

(7) 为预防起见，纸箱必须用金属带来捆绑以确保安全。

(8) 商品必须用塑料袋包装之后再装入纸箱，这是最为重要的。

V. Translate the following letter into English.

尊敬的马克先生：

第 JB-568 号合同项下的由“顺风”号货轮运来 1000 箱罐装蘑菇食品已安全抵达我处并且状态良好。

然而，虽然货物质地优良，但是我方觉得内包装太过平常了，与我们的预期尚有很大的差距。你也许了解过，有许多牌子的相同产品在本地销售，竞争非常激烈。所以希望能在下一次合作中，你方可以改进内包装，增强产品的竞争力。

盼复。

诚挚问候

2007 年 3 月 29 日

VI. Writhing

Write a letter to entrust a customer with agency, with the following given particulars.

(1) 有兴趣与对方签订购买男士衬衫的订单。

(2) 希望对方能采用新颖的内包装，增强产品的美观度。

(3) 外包装方面，建议将衬衫装入防水塑料袋里，再装入纸板箱，然后一打装一纸箱。每个纸箱里有防水衬，外有绳子加固，以防货物受潮。

(4) 请回复，告知是否同意。

Unit 6 Transport

Objective

- Understanding and writing the letters connected with transport
- Reading and understanding the relative documents

Requirement

- Getting a knowledge of the relative documents
- Grasping the usual usage of professional words and sentences
- Grasping the professional terms of transport

Introduction

Transport is an important branch of international business. As, basically, some 98% of world trade is conveyed by sea transport, exporters and importers are more concerned with transport by sea than in other ways. Transport by air is, however, increasing and is the best method for certain types of export and import, especially under emergency, though its limitation is obvious.

Cargo transported by container ships is a modern way of transportation. In recent years, combined transport, which is a road-sea-rail carriage, is a "door to door" service.

When goods are transported by road, rail or air, the contract of carriage takes the form of a Consignment Note or Airway Bill. In sea transport, chartering of ships or booking shipping space is involved. The contract between the ship owner and shipper may take the form of either a Charter Party or a Bill of Lading.

There are three parties in most movements of goods, the consignor who sends the goods, the carrier who carries them and the consignee who receives them at the destination.

Specimen Letters

1. Chartering Ships and Reply

a. Chartering Ships

Dear Sirs,

We wish to charter a ship of about two thousand tons for a single voyage from Liverpool, Britian to Shanghai, China for bulldozers.

We shall give 40 days definite notice of cargo readiness and expect the ship to be at Liverpool on June 30th ready to take cargo on board.

Please let us know whether you can arrange this for us and, if so, on what terms.

Yours faithfully,

b. Broker's Reply

Dear Sirs,

Thank you for your enquiring of March 2nd and are pleased to inform you that we have been given an option on m.v. King.This is a heavy lifter of 2,000 tons gross. The terms provisionally agreed at ￡70 per ton.

The ship can be ready for loading at Liverpool at 30 days definite notice around June. Please fax if you wish us to conclude a voyage charter for you.

Yours faithfully,

c. Charterer's Confirmation

Dear Sirs,

We received your letter of yesterday and are pleased to confirm the fax we sent this morning as follows:

Will you please make arrangements to charter this ship on the terms mentioned in your letter, namely £70 per ton, and send us the Charter Party for signature and your account commission.

Yours faithfully,

2. Booking Shipping Containers and Reply

a. Booking Shipping Containers

Dear Sirs,

We have 70 cases of canned beef for dispatch to any EMP, and shall be glad if you will arrange for your shipping container to collect them. Each weighs 75 kgs. As our client requires us to ship the goods not later than October 25th, please quote us for a shipping container from Dalian to the above mentioned port before that deadline.

Your early quotation will be highly appreciated.

Yours faithfully,

b. Reply

Thank you for your enquiry of July 1st, asking us to quote shipping container to any EMP for 70 cases of canned beef .

The shipping containers we provide are of two sizes , which are both watertight and airtight and can be loaded and locked at the factory, if necessary.

We enclose a copy of our tariff and look forward to receiving your instructions.

Yours faithfully,

3. Urging of Immediate Shipment

Dear Sirs,

We wish to draw your attention to our Order No.6557 covering 4, 000 pieces of sweater, for which we issued in your favor about 20 days ago an irrevocable L/C with expiration date on July 20th.

Our retailers are badly in need of the goods as the season is rapidly approaching. Any delay in shipping our order will undoubtedly result in big trouble.

To enable our retailers to catch the brisk demand at the start of the season, we shall be very much obliged if you effect shipment in time.

Yours faithfully,

4. Request for Extending L/C and Reply

a. Request for Extending L/C

Dear Sirs,

Re：L/C No.SM239

We are sorry to advise you that the recent floods damaged part of the railway from our factory to the port of shipment, causing some delay in making delivery of the goods under your order No. 6557.

The authorities concerned say that they are doing rush repairs and the transportation is expected to return to normal in August.

As this is the case, we hereby request you to extend your L/C No. SM239 for one month, that is, shipment date to August 20th and validity to September 10th.

Many thanks for your cooperation.

Yours faithfully,

b. Reply

Dear Sirs,

Re：L/C No. SM239

We regret to learn the present trouble you are involved in, from your letter of July 5th.

As the matter stands, we have to allow you a one-month extension of our L/C.

The delay of delivery will greatly inconvenience us. Therefore, it is important that the shipment be made within the extended time limit. We will not stand any further delay.

Yours faithfully,

5. Asking for Transshipment and Reply

a. Asking for Transshipment

Dear Sirs,

We are in receipt of the letter of credit No.3001 you established through the Barclays Bank,

London on March 6th, covering our contract No.L2007.

On perusal, We find that the Port of Destination should be Belfast and no transshipment is allowed. Since there are only one or two direct steamers monthly from Dalian to Belfst, we usually have to make shipment via Hong Kong. In order to make sure that the goods will be duly delivered, which is to our mutual benefit, we request that you amend the said L/C to allow us transshipment.

In case the above amendment is not agreeable to you, you may change the Port of Destination Belfast to Liverpool because there are more direct steamers available from Dalian to Liverpool.

Your kind acknowledgement will be highly obliged.

Yours faithfully,

b. Reply

Dear Sirs,

Our L/C No.S3001

We hasten to answer your letter dated March 17th and express our regret that we have troubled for our oversight in opening our L/C No.S3001.

This morning, we have faxed our bankers to make an amendment. On receipt of notification of the amendment issued by the bank, please arrange for the shipment with all speed. If the goods turn out to our satisfaction, we will place a repeat order with you in the near future.

Yours faithfully,

4. Shipping Instructions

Dear Sirs,

With refererence to our order No. 335 for two machine tools,we are glad to inform you that a letter of credit in your favor has been opened yesterday. We have booked shipping space on m.v. Stars which is due to sail from London to Hong kong around the end of next month. Please get the goods ready for shipment at an early date and try your utmost to ship them by that vessel without delay.

We would like to remind you that the machines must be packed in special crates with reinforced bottom. Meanwhile, please see to it that the shipping marks indicated in our order and the gross and net weight be stenciled on each crate.

We trust that the above instructions are clear to you and the shipment will give our users entire satisfaction.

Yours faithfully,

5. Shipping Advice

Dear Sirs,

We are pleased to inform you that the goods under your Contract No.DF8030 have now been shipped by s.s. Changqing,which is scheduled to sail from Jinzhou on May 20th to Hamburg.

We are sending you under cover one set of duplicate shipping documents as follows, so that you may make all the necessary preparations to take the delivery of the goods when they duly arrive at your port.

Invoice No.GW-235

Packing list No.GW-175

Certificate of origin No.654

Non-negotiable bill of lading No.FM-637

Insurance Policy No.3301

Survey Report No.KD 402

We hope this shipment will reach you in perfect condition and look forward to your further order.

Yours faithfully,

Encl.a/s

Relative Documents

1. Bill of Lading

CODE NAME CONGENBILL EDITION 1994 BILL OF LADING B/L No.

Shipper

TO BE USED WITH CHARTER PARTIES

Reference No.

consigee

COPY

NONNEGOTIABLE

notify party

vessel port of loading

port of discharge

Shipper's decription of goods

Gross weight
G.W.:
N.W:

(of which on deck at Shipper's risk: the carrier not being responsible for loss or damage however arising)

Freight payable as per CHARTER-PARTY dated____________________ Freight payable as per CHARTER-PARTY dated FREIGHT ADVANCE. Received on account of freight: _______________________________________ Time used for loading_______days ________hours.	SHIPPED at the Port of Loading in apparent good order and part of Discharge or so near thereto as she may satoly get the goods specified above. Weight, measure, quality, condition, contents and value unkown. IN WITHESS whereof the Master or Agent of the said Vessel has signed the number of Bills of Lading Indicated all of this tenor and date. Any one of which being accomplishied the others shall be valid. FOR CONDITIONS OF CARRIAGE (SEE OVER-LEAF)

Freight payable at	Place and date of issue
NumNumber of original Bs/L	Signature

Printed and Sold by S. STRAKED & SONS LtD.
23 A Line Strect. London. E. C.3
By Authority or the Baltie & International Maritime Council
Conference
Copenhagen

2. Inspection Certificate

中华人民共和国吉林省进出口商品检验局

JILIN IMPORT & EXPORT COMMODITY INSPECTION copy

BUREAU OF THE PEOPLE'S REPUBLIC OF CHINA

地址：长春云飞路 156 号

Address: 156,Yun Fei Road,

Changchun

检 验 证 书 No.

传真： (86)43126690888 日期

Fax: (86)43126690888 **INSPECTION CERTIFICATE** Date

电话：(86)43126690857

Tel. (86)43126690857

发 货 人：

Consignor--

收 货 人：

Consignee--

品 名 标记及号码

Commodity-------------------------------------- Mark & No.--

报验数量/重量：

Quantity/Weight

Declared---

检验结果：

RESULTS OF INSPECTION：

主任检验员

Chief Inspector

3. Shipping Advice

LIAOYANG CHEMICALS (GROUP) CORPORATION
LIAOYANG CITY, LIAONING PROVINCE, CHINA
Tel.: (86)4193746122 Fax: (86)4193746333

SHIPPING ADVICE

DATE:NOV,18,2006

TO: PANTZU INTERNATIONAL PETLTD
333LIEN STREET TOR25-07 FAR EASTERN BAND BUILDING SINGAPORE 534478
FAX: 37 6624448

DEAR SIRS,

WE ARE PLEASED TO ADVISE YOU THAT SHIPMENT OF FERTILIZER IN BAGS HAS BEEN ATTANGED AS FOLLOWS:

NAME OF VESSEL:BLUEKEE
BILL OF LADING NO.:LY43227
COMMODITY: FERTILIZER IN BAGS
PACKING:IN 60KG NEW WOVEN POLYPROPYLENE BAGS WITH POLYETHYLENE INNER LINER. 1 PERCENT EMPTY BAGS TO BE SUPPLIED FREE OF CHARGE.
MARKING: AS PER BUYER'S MARKING
QUANTITY: 226198 BAGS
NET WEIGHT: 13,571.880 MT
GROSS WEIGHT: 13628.375 MT
VALUE OF GOODS:USD 1,453,454.5 FOB ST DALIAN PORT, CHINA
COUNTRY OF ORIGIN: CHINA
PORT OF SHIPMENT:DALIAN PORT, CHINA
PORT OF DISCHARGE: COLOMBO, SRILANKA
ETD LOADING PORT:NOV,15 ,2006
ETA DESTINATION: DEC,15,2006

VERY TRULY YOURS,
LIAOYANG
CHEMICALS(GROUP)CORPORATION

____

AUTHORIZED SIGNATURE

4. Certificate of Quantity/Weight

We, Varian B.V, Herculesweg 8,4338PL Middelburg, The Netherlands, being the manufacturer, hereby certify that the CP3800Gas chromatograph system, Serial No.CP941220 has been supplied in the quantity according to the attachment for Contract No. 2003LHIE-LT90 and weight as specified in our Packing List No.311097167.The quantity and packing have been checked before shipment.

5. Certificate of Origin

<table>
<tr><td colspan="2">ORIGINAL</td></tr>
<tr><td>1.Exporter</td><td>Certificate No.</td></tr>
<tr><td></td><td rowspan="2">CERTIFICATE OF ORIGIN
OF
THE PEOPLE'S REPUBLIC OF CHINA</td></tr>
<tr><td>2.Consignee</td></tr>
<tr><td>3.Means of transport and route</td><td>5.For certifying authority use only</td></tr>
<tr><td colspan="2">4.Country / region of destination</td></tr>
</table>

6.Marks and numbers	7.Number and kind of packages; description of goods	8.H.S.Code	9.Quantity	10.Number and date of invoices

<table>
<tr><td>11.Declaration by the exporter
The undersigned hereby declares that the above details and statements are correct, that all the goods were produced in China and that they comply with the Rules of Origin of the People's Republic of China</td><td>12.Certification
It is hereby certified that the declaration by the exporter is correct.</td></tr>
<tr><td>Place and date, signature and stamp of authorized signatory</td><td>Place and date, signature and stamp of certifying authority</td></tr>
</table>

6. Commercial invoice

<table>
<tr><td colspan="5">SHANGHAI FOREIGN TRADE CORP.
SHANGHAI, CHINA</td></tr>
<tr><td colspan="5">COMMERCIAL INVOICE</td></tr>
<tr><td colspan="4" rowspan="4">To:</td><td>Invoice No.:</td></tr>
<tr><td>Invoice Date:</td></tr>
<tr><td>S/C No.:</td></tr>
<tr><td>S/C Date:</td></tr>
<tr><td colspan="2">From:</td><td colspan="3">To:</td></tr>
<tr><td colspan="2">Letter of Credit No.:</td><td colspan="3">Issued By:</td></tr>
<tr><td>Marks and Numbers</td><td>Number and kind of package
Description of goods</td><td>Quantity</td><td>Unit Price</td><td>Amount</td></tr>
<tr><td></td><td></td><td></td><td></td><td></td></tr>
<tr><td>TOTAL:</td><td colspan="4"></td></tr>
<tr><td>SAY TOTAL:</td><td colspan="4"></td></tr>
</table>

Notes

1. shipping n. 装运，船运，运输
   shipping documents 装运单据
   one set of shipping documents mainly includes：
      bill of lading 提单
      commercial invoice 发票
      certificate of quality 质量证明书
      certificate of quantity 重量证明书
      insurance policy 保险单
      weight memo 重量单

shipping agent　装运代理人，发货代理人

shipping company　船运公司

shipping order　装货单，下货纸

shipping instruction　装运指示，装运须知

shipping weight　启运重量

shipping space　舱位，载位，船位

shipping advice　装船通知

2. carriage　n. 运载

carrier　n. 承运人

3. consignor　n. 托运人，发货人

consignee　n. 收货人

4. consignment note　铁路运单

5. airway bill　空运单

6. charter party　租船契约

7. voyage charter　航次

8. combined transport　联运

9. booking note　订舱单

10. specifications　规格(复数)

11. forwarding agent　运输行，运输商

12. EMP　European Main Ports　欧洲主要口岸，按照航运工会统一规定，EMP 包括意大利的热那亚(Genoa)，法国的马赛(Marseilles)，比利时的安特卫普(Antwerp)，荷兰的鹿特丹(Rotterdam)，英国的伦敦(London)，德国的汉堡(Hamburg)，丹麦的哥本哈根(Copenhagen)等港口。

13. watertight　adj. 防水的

14. airtight　adj. 不漏气的，密封的

15. freight　n. 货物(特指装载于车、船、飞机上的)；运费

freight charges　运费

freight agency　运货代理商

freight forwarder　运输公司

freight rate　运费率

freight service　货运

16. tariff　n. 运费表；关税；关税率
tariff compact　关税协定
tariff elimination　关税减让
tariff quota　关税限额
tariff rate　关税率
17. expiration date　截止，到期
18. packing list　装箱单
19. certificate of origin　原产地证明
20. non-negotiable bill of lading　提单副本
original bill of lading　正本提单
21. insurance policy　保险单
22. survey report　检验报告
23. in duplicate　一式两份
in triplicate　一式三份
in quadruplicate　一式四份
in quintuplicate　一式五份
in four　(five,six,…)copies 一式四(五、六……)份
24. take delivery of　提货
make delivery of　发货
25. be scheduled to　预计，预期
26. m.v. 也可记作 M/V　motor vessel　内燃机船
s.s. 等于 S/S　steam ship　轮船
m.s.　motor ship　内燃机船
27. shipping mark　装运唛头(商标)
唛头实例：
ABC……………………… 主要标志(通常为发货人或收货人名城的缩写或代号)
Contract No.A 965 ………. 合同号码(也可为订单号码，运单号码，许可证号码等)
Nos.2-5…………………… 件号标志(表示该箱为全部五箱货物中第二箱)
SYDNEY .... 目的地标志(如需转船，还应列上转运地名如，SYDNEY)
10* 8* 6ft………………… 体积标志
G300KGS …………………重量标志
MADE IN HONG KONG…原产地标志

Exercises

I. Fill in the blanks with prepositions and then translate the following into Chinese.

(1) ______ ______Order No.8088 the goods have been ready ______ shipment ______quite some time.

(2) We wish to draw your attention ______the fact that the date ______delivery is approaching, but ______ ______the present moment, we have not receive any news ______you.

(3) ______receipt ______your cable of April 11, we at once request the bank of China ______London to establish a letter of credit ______your favor ______pounds sterling ______the amount ______ $ 30,000.

(4) Our terms ______payment are irrevocable letter of credit, which we have agreed during the negotiation.

(5) Please make sure that the stipulations______ the L/C are______exact accordance ______the terms ______ the sales contract.

(6) ______accordance ______ the terms ______ payment as stipulated ______the contract, please establish L/C ______ fifteen days______ receipt______ our delivery notice, an irrevocable letter of credit______ our favour.

(7) We are ______ receipt ______ your letter______ Sept.19 enclosing catalogues and price list______ bicycles and sewing machines.

(8) S/S"East Wind" is due to sail______Shanghai______London______23rd ______ November.

(9) Owing______ the delay______ the part______ the suppliers, we must ask you to extend the date______ shipment______ September 10th ______ October 10th.

(10) ______receipt______ your amendment______L/C No.378, we shall immediately make shipment______ the goods.

II. Fill in the blanks of the following letter.

Dear sirs,

As there are no direct steamers ______for your port within the time of shipment ______stipulated in your letter of credit, we would suggest that you ______ your credit to allow_____, so that the goods______ by you can be shipped by the first______ steamer with transshipment, instead of waiting______ for a direct steamer. We would like to state that goods dispatched______ transshipment will, at least in your case, most probably______ you earlier to meet your urgent needs.

We await with keen interest your______ to the L/C.

Yours faithfully,

III. Choose the appropriate words to fill in the blanks.

Forward; sai; option; expedite; find; advise; note; transshipment; comply; destination; allow; ship

(1) We will do our best to______shipment to meet your requirements in time.

(2) We shall______you by cable as soon as the goods are shipped.

(3) We have the pleasure to inform you that the shipment has gone______per s.s. "Liaohe" and hope that it will arrive at the ______in perfect condition.

(4) We are pleased to inform you that 4,000 dozen shirts under Sales Confirmation No.K145,L/C NO.739 have gone off on S/S Beijing, which_____on September 12 for Dubai.Enclosed pleased ______a set or duplicate copies of shipping documents.

(5) The shipment time is June or July at our ______and the goods will be shipped in one lot.

(6) Because there is no direct steamer from here to your port, we suggest that you accept ______at Hong Kong.

(7) According to the shipping schedule, it will be impossible for us to ship the goods until the end of November, which please ______.

(8) We regret our inability to ______with your request for shipping the goods in early November, because the direct steamer sailing for your port calls at our port only around November 20.

(9) As the manufacturers cannot get all the quantity ready at the same time, it is necessary for the contract stipulations to be so worded as to ______partial shipment.

(10) The cargo has been ______ on s.s. Beijing for transshipment at Hong Kong per s.s. Taishan.

IV. Choose the right word to complete the sentences.

(1) We Will do our best to________ shipment to meet your requirements in time.

A. comply　　B. make　　C. expedite　　D. arrange

(2) Passenger liners often take a certain amount of________.

A. cargoes B. cargo C. shipments D. quantities

(3) We have the pleasure to inform you that the shipment has gone________per s.s. East Wind and hope that it will arrive at the destination in ________condition.

A.on, good B. for, complete C. forward, perfect D. onto, perfect

(4) The shipment time is May or June at our________ and the goods will be shipped in one________.

A. choice, shipment B. option, lot

C. decision, cargo D. option, consignment

(5) We regret our inability to________with your request for shipping the goods in early July.

A. compliance B. comply C. manage D.arrange

(6) Before deciding which form of transport to use, a ________ will take into account the factors of cost, speed and safety.

A. consignor B. consignee C. shipper D. shipowner

(7) Any loss of damage noticed when the goods are delivered must be reported to the________ at the time, otherwise he will not be liable for it.

A. carrier B. shipper C. consignee D. consignor

(8) They intended to lower the cost of the products, ________ they did not succeed in reducing the package costs.

A. therefore B. and C. however D. furthermore

(9) As the _______ of the goods was not strong enough to withstand the rough sea voyage, shipment was withhold at the last minute in order to give time for ________ improvement.

A. pack, packet B. package, packing

C. package, packaging D. packing, packaging

(10) Since three fifths of the voyage is in tropical weather and the goods are liable to go mouldy, we think it advisable to have the shipment ________ the risk of mould.

A. covered insurance B. taken out insured

C. covered against D. insured for

V. Translate the following into English.

(1) 信用证 LN358 号因无直达轮，请允许改转船。

(2) 我们急需化肥，请你方将标题所指的合同项下 5 万吨月内装完。

(3) 情况既然这样，我们做好一切准备，等候你方船只来我港。

(4) 如果可能的话，请立即装“腾飞”轮，4 月 4 日由大连起航。

(5) 收到信用证后，请立即安排装运。

(6) 你方倘能在本月底之前把货物设法运出，我们将十分感谢。

(7) 上述合同项下各货，现已备妥待运，请点开信用证以便我们早日装运。

(8) 货物也已备妥待运，正在与轮船公司洽办装 “飞云”轮，预定 10 月 15 日左右从青岛开航。

(9) 如果你方信用证的电报期通知 3 天内到达这里，货物便可以在本月内装上“天安”轮运走。

(10) 由于你方信用证条款与我们销售确认书的条款不一致，货物不能装船。

VI. Translate the following into Chinese.

(1) It is important that the goods be completed for delivery as stipulated in the L/C, say by August 30th. If not, you should be responsible for any loss that might be caused by the delay of shipment.

(2) For the goods under our Contract No.8667 we have booked space on s.s. “Happiness” due to arrive in London around October 25th. Please communicate with Weidi Co.,Ltd, Beijing, our shipping agents, for loading arrangements.

VII. Writing.

Write a letter, asking a shipping agent to collect a consignment from your warehouse and make all arrangements for transportation to Cairo. Give imaginary particulars as to name of commodity, names of consignor and consignee and say who will take delivery of the consignment upon arrival.

Unit 7 Terms of Payment

Objective

- Understanding and writing the letters connected with payment
- Reading and understanding the relative documents

Requirement

- Get a knowledge of the relative documents
- Grasping the usual usage of professional words and sentences
- Grasping the professional terms of payment

Introduction

Settlement of the purchase price in foreign trade is realized by collection and payment of foreign exchange. In every contract for the sales of goods abroad, the clause dealing with the payment of the purchase price embodies four elements: time, mode, place and currency of payment.

Terms of payment are different.Terms of payment define the conditions under which the seller and buyer agree to settle the financial amount of the sales contract. The basic points are: method of payment; amount; place and date of payment; method of remittance; cost relating to the payment.

International business transactions are much more complicated than domestic ones. The payment process is much longer, and involves all kinds of risks.

The method of payment for each transaction is to be agreed upon between the two trading parties at the time of placing an order. The most often adopted method of payment in our foreign trade is payment by the letter of credit.

Specimen Letters

1. Buyer Instructs Bank and the Bank's Reply

a. Buyer Instructs Bank

Dear Sirs,

We enclose an application form for documentary credit and shall be glad if you will arrange to open for our account with your office in London an irrevocable letter of credit for &500,000 in favour of the Urban Trading Company, the credit to be valid until November 30th.

The credit which evidences shipment of 2, 000 tons of steels may be used against presentation of the following documents: Bill of Lading in triplicate, one copy of each Commercial Invoice, Packing List, Certificate of Insurance and Certificate of Origin. The company may draw on your London office at 60 d/s for each shipment.

Yours faithfully,

b. the Bank Agrees to Open Credit

Dear Sirs,

As instructed in your letter of May 2nd, we are arranging to open a letter of credit with our office in London in favor of the Urban Trading Company, valid until November 30th.

Please check our enclosed telex opening the credit to ensure that it agrees with your instructions. As soon as the credit is used we shall debit your account with the amount notified to us as having been drawn against the L/C.

We shall see to it that your instructions are carefully carried out.

Yours faithfully,

2. The Buyer Notifies the Seller and the Seller's Reply

a. Buyer Notifies Seller

Dear Sirs,

We are glad to inform you that we have opened today an irrevocable L/C No.226311 in your favour for USD 30,000 with Bank of China, (Hong Kong) Limited, …(followed by the address) valid until May 25th, 2005. Bank of China, Beijing Branch …(followed by the address) will be the Advising Bank.

The L/C authorizes you to draw at sight on the Bank after shipment is made. Please present the following documents：

(1) Signed Commercial Invoice in three originals

(2) Packing List in triplicate

(3) Full set of Original Bill of Lading showing "to order" and blank endorsed, marked "freight collect" notifying Global Forwarder, 246 Lin Kong Road, Shatin, New Territories, HK SAR, Tel：23677788, Fax: 23677798 .

(4) Photocopy of Certificate of Origin issued by the public authorities of China.

Global Forwarder will act as our forwarding agent. They will deal with marking and dispatch shipping instructions. Please contact them about shipping matters and fax us once the goods have been shipped. We shall expect your consignment by May.

Yours faithfully,

b. Seller's Reply

Dear Sirs,

We thank you for the L/C for this business, of which we have been notified today by the Bank of China, Beijing Branch.

We are heavily committed for the fourth quarter. But with an eye to our long-term friendly relationship, we assure you the prompt delivery so that these commodities will catch your business season.

Yours faithfully,

3. Exporter Presents Documents

Dear Sirs,

Referring to your advice of May 10th, we enclose shipping documents for the consignment of 2, 000 tons of steels to Browning &Sons.

As required by them we have included all charges in our invoice, which amounts to &500,000 and enclose our draft at 60 days' for this sum. We shall be glad if, after acceptance you will discount it at the current rate and remit the net amount to our account with the Bank of England.

We thank you for your help in this matter.

Yours faithfully,

4. Bank Debits Buyer

Dear Sirs,

As instructed by your letter of May 12th, our London office have just accepted for your account a bill for &500,000 drawn by the Urban Trading Company for the consignment of 2, 000 tons of steels to you by m.v. "Star". We have debited your account with this amount and our charges amounting to &500.

The vessel left London on October 3th and it due to arrive in Hong kong on November 4th. The shipping documents for the consignment are now with us and we shall be glad if you will arrange to collect them.

Yours faithfully,

5. Urging Establishment of L/C

Dear Sirs,

<u>Our Sales Confirmation No. 043 covering your Order No. 311</u>

Further to our letter of February 2nd urging you to establish the L/C, we are very disappointed to say that we have not received any news from you.

We would like to remind you that it is stipulated in our Sales Confirmation that shipment should be effected during March. The goods concerned have been ready for shipment for quite some time. If we do not receive your L/C by the end of February we are sorry to say we shall not be able to make shipment within the stipulated time.

We hope this matter will receive your prompt attention.

Yours faithfully,

6. The Seller's Request for Amendment of L/C

a. Ask for Transshipment and Partial Shipments

Dear Sirs,

Your L/C No. 8900

We have received the captioned letter of credit covering the shipment of 3,000 tons of Steel. On examination, we find transshipment and partial shipment are not allowed.

As direct sailings to your port are infrequent, we have to ship via Rotterdam more often than not. We can expedite delivery if we can ship immediately the goods we have in stock instead of waiting for the whole lot to be completed. As a result, transshipment and partial shipments are necessary. Therefore, we are asking you to amend your L/C to read "partial shipments and transshipment allowed."

Please confirm the amendments by fax so that we may arrange shipment accordingly. We shall appreciate it if you will modify promptly the L/C as requested.

Yours faithfully,

b. Ask for Cancelling Manufacturer's Certificate

Dear Sirs,

Re：Your Letter of Credit No. 5454

We have received your captioned Letter of Credit among the clause specified in your credit, we find that the following two points do not conform to the relative contract：

(1) Your credit calls for Manufacturer's Certificate, which is not included in the contract. In fact, the contracted commodity is a kind of agricultural product. It is impossible to obtain a manufacturer's certificate.

(2) The contract number is 04/1245 instead of 03/1245.

As the goods are now ready for shipment, you are requested to amend your credit as soon as possible.

Yours truly,

c. Ask for Extension

Dear Sirs,

Re: Your L/C No. AG4582

We have received your L/C No. AG4582 for the amount of $ 2, 950 to cover your Order No. 860 for 20 metric tons of cotton.

The said credit calls for shipment on or before December 31st. As the earliest steamer sailing for your port is S/S "PEACE" scheduled to leave Shanghai on or about January 3rd next year, it is, therefore, impossible for us to effect shipment at the time you named.

This being the case, We have to ask you to extend the date of shipment to January 15th, under advice to us by fax.

Yours faithfully,

7. Collection

a. Shipping Company Sends Invoice

Dear Sirs,

We enclose our invoice No. 56A/85. Please remit the amount due as per agreement.

Yours faithfully,

Enc.

(Invoice No. 56A/85)

b. Charter's Reply

Dear Sirs,

We have received your letter of April 5th enclosing Invoice No. 56A/85 for the freight for 2, 000 tons of steels shipped by m.v. Star. The statement has been checked and found correct and we have instructed our banker to make remittance accordingly.

We apologize for the underpayment of US$ 230.00 on your Invoice No. 65A/85. This was due to a misreading of the amount due. The final figure was not very clearly printed and we regrettably read it as US$ 8, 000.00 instead of US$ 8, 230.00.

Yours faithfully,

8. Requesting Payment by D/P and Reply

a. Requesting Payment by D/P

Dear Sirs,

Re：Our order 375 for your Stockings

Further to our letter of June 1st regarding your Stockings, we would like to make payment on D/P basis.

We propose this method of payment as the value of the order is less than US $ 3,000 and we can save the expense of opening a letter of credit. We believe this will help our sales. We hope you will accommodate us in this respect and agree to our arrangement for payment.

We look forward to receiving your confirmation of our order.

Yours faithfully,

b. Accepting Payment by D/P

Dear Sirs,

Re：Your order 375 for our Stockings

We have received your letter of June 7th requesting to make payment by D/P for the captioned goods.

We agree to your proposal. However, we consider it advisable to make it clear that for future transaction D/P can only be accepted if the amount involved is below US $ 3,000 or its equivalent in RMB at the conversion rate then prevailing. If the amount exceeds that figure, payment by Letter of Credit will be required.

We would like to say we extend you this accommodation only in the light of our long business relations. We sincerely hope we can enlarge the business to our mutual benefit.

Yours faithfully,

9. Urging Payment

Dear Sirs,

Account No.8756

Not having received any reply to our E-mail of September 8th requesting settlement of the above account, we are writing again to remind you that the amount still owing is US $ 80,000. No doubt there is some special reason for delay in payment and we should welcome an explanation and also your remittance,

Yours faithfully,

Relative Documents

1. Application Form for Documentary Credit

开立不可撤销跟单信用证申请书

<table>
<tr><td colspan="4">IRREVOCABLE DOCUMENTARY CREDIT APPLICATION
TO：
No.　　　　Date：Jul.21.,2006</td></tr>
<tr><td colspan="2">Applicant
Tel：
Fax：</td><td colspan="2">Beneficiary(full name, address and tel etc.)
TEL：
FAX：</td></tr>
<tr><td>Partial shipments
(×) allowed ( )not allowed</td><td colspan="2">Transhipment
(×)allowed ( ) not allowed</td><td>issued by (×) teletransmission
( )express delivery</td></tr>
<tr><td colspan="2">Loading on board/dispatch/ taking in charge at/from
PORT
Not later than AUG.10, 2004
For transportation to SHANGHAI, CHINA</td><td colspan="2">Contract No.：SMST/24116
Credit Amount (both in figures and words)：
USD________
US DOLLARS______________________ ONLY.
Trade Term：( )FOB (×) CFR ( ) CIF ( ) Others：</td></tr>
<tr><td colspan="2" rowspan="2">Description of goods：
SEE ATTACHMENT</td><td colspan="2">Date and place of expiry：Aug.30., 2004 CHINA</td></tr>
<tr><td colspan="2">Credit available with
( ) by sight payment
(×) by acceptance
( ) by negotiation
( ) by deferred payment at
against the documents detailed herein
(×) and beneficiary's draft for 100% of invoice value
at 90 DAYS AFTER B/L DATE On issuing bank</td></tr>
</table>

Documents required：(marked with ×)
1. (×) Signed commercial invoice in 3 copies indicating L/C No. and Contract No. SMST/24116.
2. (×) Full set of clean on board Bills of Lading made out [×] to order/ [ ] to the order of and blank endorsed, marked " freight [×] prepaid/ [ ] to collect showing freight amount" notifying [ ]the applicant./ [ ]
3. ( ) Air Waybills showing "freight [ ]prepaid/ [ ] to collect indicating freight amount" and consigned to
4. ( )Insurance Policy/Certificate in 3 copies for 110% of the invoice value showing claims payable in China in currency of the draft, blank endorsed, covering ([ ] Ocean Marine Transportation / [ ] Air Transportation / [ ] Over Land Transportation) All Risks, War Risks. / [ ]
5. (×) Packing list / Weight Memo in 3 copies indicating
6. (×) Certificate of Quantity/Weight in 3 copies issued by [×] manufacturer/[ ] Seller/[ ]independent surveyor at the loading port, indicating the actual surveyed quantity / weight of shipped goods as well as the packing condition.
7. (×) Certificate of Quality in 3 copies issued by [×] manufacturer / [ ] public recognized surveyor. / [ ]
8. (×) Beneficiary's Certified copy of fax dispatched to the applicant within 2 days after ship ment advising the contract number, name of commodity, quantity, invoice value, bill of loading, bill of loading date, the ETA date and shipping Co.
9. ( ) Beneficiary's Certificate certifying that extra copies of the documents have been dispatched to the [ ] application. [ ]
10. ( ) Certificate of Origin in copies certifying.
Ⅱ. ( )Other documents, if any：Additional instruction：(marked with ×)
1. (×)All banking charges outside the opening bank are for beneficiary's account.
2. (×)Documents must be presented within 21 days after the date of issuance of the transport documents but within the validity of this credit.
3. ( ) Third party as shipper is not acceptable, Short Form / Blank B/l is not acceptable.
4. ( ) Both quantity and amount more or less are allowed.
5. (×) All documents to be forwarded in one lot by express unless otherwise stated above.
6. ( ) Other terms, if any.

For banks use only	我公司承担本申请书背面所列责任及承诺，并保证按照办理。
Seal and / or Signature checked by ( )L/C Margin % checked by ( ) Credit Facility checked by ( ) Ent ( ) Ver ( ) App ( ) Date：	(申请人名称及印签章) RMB A/C No. USD or ( ) A/C No. 联系人： 电话：

form Customs and Practice for Documentary Credit (1993 Revision) ICC Publication No. 500.

ATTACHMENT

NAME OF COMMODITY QUANTITY UNIT PRICE TOTAL AMOUNT

HDPEGRADE NO.9004 204MT USD937.00/MT CIF SHANGHAI USD191148.00

HDPEGRADE NO.3234 198MT USD927.00/MT CIF SHANGHAI USD183546.00

2. Irrevocable Documentary L/C

FAR EAST NATIONAL BANK OF SAN FRANCISCO
CALIFORNIA U.S.A.

IRREVOCABLE DOCUMENTARY CREDIT	L/C NUMBER：FENB41170 DATE OF ISSUE：MAY 30th 2, 005,SAN FRANCISCO
EXPIRY DATE AND PLACE： JULY 30th, 2005, NANJING	Applicant： DOUBLE EAGLE IMP AND EXP COMPANY 235 MONTGOMERY STREET,SUITE 1015 SAN FRANCISCO CA94104 U.S.A.
Beneficiary: NANJING CLOTH FLOWERS CO., LTD. 400 SHANGHAI ROAD, NANJING CHINA	Amount: USD15,220.00(United States Dollars) FIFTEEN THOUSAND TWO HUNDRED AND TWENTY ONLY.
AVAILABLE BY：BENEFICIARY'S DRAFTS AT SIGHT DRAWN ON US	
SHIPMENT DETAILS： FROM SHANGHAI TO SAN FRANCISCO LATEST ON 30 JUN 2001 CIF SAN FRANCISCO U.S.A. PARTIAL SHIPMENTS：NOT ALLOWED TRANSHIPMENT：ALLOWED	

DESCRIPTION OF GOODS：3 ITEMS OF PLUSH TOYS AS PER SALES CONTRACT NO. JTC-DE073 DATED MARCH 15th 2001

DOCUMENTS REQUIRED：

SIGNED COMMERCIAL INVOICE IN TRIPLICATE INDICATING SEPERATELY FOB VALUE, FREIGHT CHARGES, INSURANCE PREMIUM AND L/C NUMBER

FULL SET ORIGINAL CLEAN ON BOARD OCEAN BILLS OF LADING MADE OUT TO SHIPPER'S ORDER, ENDORSED TO THE ORDER OF FAR EAST NATIONAL BANK OF SAN FRANCISCO, MARKED FREIGHT PREPAID AND NOTIFY APPLICANT MENTIONING THIS L/C NUMBER

MARINE INSURANCE POLICY OR CERTIFICATE FOR FULL CIF VALUE PLUS 10% COVERING CIC ALL RISKS AND WAR RISKS.

PACKING LIST IN TRIPLICATE

CERTIFICATE OF ORIGIN

DETAILS OF CHARGES：ALL BANKING CHARGES AT YOUR END ARE FOR ACCOUNT OF BENEFICIARY

+PERIOD FOR PRESENTATION：DOCUMENTS TO BE PRESENTED WITHIN 10 DAYS AFTER THE B/L DATE

+INSTRUCTION TO PRESENTING BANK：DOCUMENTS ARE TO BE DESPATCHED BY REGISTERED AIRMAIL IN ONE COVER

THIS CREDIT IS SUBJECT TO UCP 500

3. Stand-By L/C 备用信用证

To：Bank of communications, SHENYANG Branch
From：XYZ BANK
Date：DECEMBER 20th 2004
Standby Letter of Credit

With reference to the loan agreement no. 2004HN028 (hereinafter referred to as "the agreement") signed between Bank of Communications, SHENYANG Branch (hereinafter referred to as "the lender") and LIAONING ABC Co., Ltd (hereinafter referred to as "the borrower")for a principal amount of RMB 2,000,000 (in words),we hereby issue our irrevocable standby letter of credit no.810LC040000027D in the lender's favor for amount of the HONG KONG AABBCC CORPORATION which has its registered office at AS 8 FL. 2SEC. CHARACTER RD. HONG KONG for an amount up to UNITED STATES DOLLARS THREE MILLION ONLY.(USD3,000,000) which covers the principal amount of the agreement plus interest occured from aforesaid principal amount and other charges all of which the borrower has undertaken to pay the lender. The exchange rate will be the buying rate of USD/RMB quoted by Bank of Communications on the date of our payment. In the case that the guaranteed amount is not sufficient to satisfy your claim due to the exchange rate fluctuation between USD and RMB, we hereby agree to increase the amount of this standby L/C accordingly.

Partial drawing and multiple drawing are allowed under this standby L/C.

This standby letter of credit is available by sight payment. We engage with you that upon receipt of your draft(s) and your signed statement or tested telex statement or SWIFT stating that the amount in USD represents the unpaid balance of indebtedness due to you by the borrower, we will pay you within 7 banking days the amount specified in your statement or SWIFT. All drafts drawn hereunder must be marked drawn under XYZ Bank standby letter of credit no. 810LC040000027D dated DECEMBER 20th, 2004.

This standby letter of is credit will come into effect on DECEMBER 20th, 2004 and expire on DECEMBER 9th, 2005 at the counter of bank of Communications, SHENYANG branch.

This standby letter of credit is subject to Uniform Customs and Practice for Document Credits (1993 revision) International Chamber of Commerce Publication No.500.

4. Revolving L/C

IRREVOCABLE REVOLVING LETTER OF CREDIT

<table>
<tr><td colspan="3">RECONSTRUCTION DEVELORPENT BANK

Telex: BHD 1142
Commercial House Telephone: 5883218
Brussels, Belgium Issued Date& place
10th January,20-
ORIGINAL Brussels</td></tr>
<tr><td>Revolving Credit Irrevocable</td><td>Issuing Bank
Credit No.
BH 0821</td><td>Advising Bank
Credit No.
2108 HB</td></tr>
</table>

Advising Bank	Applicant
Trust Development Bank Commercial Centre, Amsterdam, Holland	Babit Machine-Making Industry Co., (Ltd.) Bavel Building, Brussels, Belgium
Beneficiary	**Amount**
Watat International Co., Ltd. Lisi Centre, Amsterdam, Holland	US$ 600,000 (Six Hundred Thousand U.S. Dollars)
This credit is issued subject to Uniform Customs and Practice for Documentary Credits 2000 Revision, ICC Publication No.500.	Date & Place of Expiry This credit remains valid in the country of beneficiary until November 10th, 20_ _ (inclusive)

AUTOMATIC CUMULATIVE REVOL VING CREDIT

TRANSMITTED THROUGH：TRUST DEVELOPMENT BANK

Dear Sir(s),

We hereby open our Irrevocable Automatic Cumulative Revolving Documentary Credit in your favour and authorize you to draw on us at sight up to an aggregate amount of US$ 600,000(U.S. dollars six hundred thousand only)per three(3) calendar months cumulative commencing with January 30th, 20_ _, revolving on the first business day of each successive month and ending with October 30th, 20_ _.

This credit is revolving for three(3) shipments only, each shipment should be effected at three months intervals, but the amount of each shipment is not exceeding US$ 200,000(U.S. dollars two hundred thousand only).

The unused balance of each shipment is cumulative to the following shipment.

The amount of this credit shall be restored automatically after date of negotiation.

Accompanied by the following documents：

1. Commercial invoice in duplicate copied, indicating contract NO.______.

2. Packing list in duplicate.

3. Full set clean shipped on board bill(s) of lading marked "Freight Prepaid"to order of shipper endorsed to Reconstruction Development Bank, notifying buyers.

Conditions of shipment;

Trans-shipment is permitted.

Partial shipments are permitted.

From Rotterdam to Antwerp.

Shipment date：Shipment is to be effected not later than October 10th 20_ _.

Covering：List of spare parts

Please see continuation sheet attached.

Special instructions：

Please see continuation sheet attached.

Undertaking clause:	Advising's Bank Notification
We hereby agree with the drawers, endorsers, and bona-fide holders of drafts drawn in compliance with the terms of the credit that such drafts shall be duly honoured on presentation and paid at maturity. Yours truly, Reconstruction Development Bank Signature______________	The amount of each draft negotiated, together with the date, must be stated on the back here of. Advising Bank Signature________________

RECONSTRUCTION DEVELORPENT BANK

Telex：BHD 1142

Commercial House Telephone：5883218

Brussels, Belgium Issued Date& place

January 10th, 20_ _

ORIGINAL

Brussels

Revolving Credit Irrevocable	Issuing Bank Credit No. BH 0821	Advising Bank Credit No. 2108 HB

Advising Bank	Applicant
Trust Development Bank Commercial Centre, Amsterdam, Holland	Babit Machine-Making Industry Co., (Ltd.) Bavel Building, Brussels, Belgium
Beneficiary	**Amount**
Watat International Co., Ltd. Lisi Centre, Amsterdam, Holland	US$ 600,000 (Six Hundred Thousand U.S. Dollars)

This attached Sheet forms an integral part of our Irrevocable

L/C No. BH 0821

CONTINUATION SHEET

Covering：List of Spare Parts(Omit)

Special Instructions：

1. Special instructions for beneficiary

April 30th, 20_ _ Despatch the original draft and documents by first mail to the bank, which is located in the country of advising bank for unrestricted negotiation.

July 30th, 20_ _ Despatch the original draft and documents by second mail to the bank,which is located in the country of advising bank for unrestricted negotiation.

October 30th, 20_ _ Despatch the original draft and documents by third mail to the bank, which is located in the country of advising bank for unrestricted negotiation.

2. Special instruction for advising bank

Despatch the certificate "Documents must strictly conform with the terms of this Credit" and drafts drawn at sight by the beneficiary on the Reconstruction Development Bank, Brussels, Belgium, for reimbursement.

3. Remark

All drafts against this Credit must be drawn and negotiated on or before (April 30th, 20_ _), (July 30th, 20_ _)and (October 30th, 20_ _).

4. Charges

All banking charges are for beneficiary's account and delivery of the L/C should be withheld pending beneficiary's agreement to pay the advising bank's charges.

____

Signature

5. Application for Amendment to L/C

APPLICATION FOR AMENDMENT TO LETTER OF CREDIT

信用证修改申请书

No.of Credit Facility： Date：

授信额度编号： 日 期：

To：China Merchants Bank　　　　　　　　　　　　　　Branch(Sub-Branch)
致：招商银行　　　　　　　　　　　　　　　　　　　　分(支)行

L/C　No.____________　　　　　　　　　　　　　　Amount：_________
信用证号码：______________　　　　　　　　　　　金　额：__________
Amendment No.
修改次数(银行填写)：

Please amend the above L/C by Swift/Telex as follows <marked with (×) >：
请以 SWIFT/电传方式修改上述信用证如下<注有(×)部分>：

(　　)　Shipment date is extended to____________
(　　)　Expiry date is extended to ____________
(　　)　Increasing credit amount by _____________to ______________

Others：
(　　)____

All other terms and conditions remain unchanged.
其余条款不变。

Charges and fees if any, are for our a/c No._________________
修改之手续费及电信费用请从我公司________________账号扣付。

Stamp and signature(s) of the applicant：
申　请　人　签　章：

银行审查意见：

经办：

复核：　　　　授权：

6. Bill of Exchange

No.36/1883

Drawn under Bank of New York, USA

L/C No.18542 dated June 4th, 2006

London, July5th, 2006

£10,000

Sixty days after sight of this First of Exchange (Second and Third of the same tenor and date being unpaid) to Bank of South Africa or order One Thousand Pounds only (English currency), value received. Payable at the current rate of exchange for Banker's sight drafts on London.

For Weavewell Woolen Co.,Ltd

(signed)

Director

To：Messrs.Strutton,

Notes

1. Letter of Credit (L/C 信用证)
   Irrevocable/ Revocable letter of credit 不可撤销的/可撤销的信用证
   Unconfirmed/ confirmed letter of credit 不可保兑的/可保兑的信用证
   Sight L/C 即期信用证
   Usance credit/time credit/term credit 远期信用证
   Documentary/ clean L/C 跟单/光票信用证
   Stand-by Letter of Credit 备用信用证
2. to send a cheque for payment 支票支付
3. remitter n. 寄款人; remittee n. 收款人
4. upon presentation of drafts 汇票提示后
   documentary bill 跟单汇票
   accommodation bill 空头汇票
   original bill 原始汇票
   renewed bill 改写票据
   sight bill; bill on demand 即期汇票

usance bill; bill at usance　远期汇票
overdue bill　逾期汇票
5. … days' after sight, after… days' sight　见票后……日付款
6. promissory note (P/N)　本票
7. letter of hypothecation　押汇负责书；押汇保证书
8. trust receipt/letter of indemnity　担保书
9. acceptance　n. 承兑
qualified acceptance　有条件承兑
partial acceptance　部分认付
dishonour　拒付，退票
dishonour by non-acceptance　拒绝承兑而退票
10. endorsement　n. 背书
general endorsement, blank endorsement　无记名背书
special endorsement, full endorsement　记名式背书
conditional endorsement　附条件背书
restrictive endorsement　限制性背书
endorsement without recourse　追索权背书
11. maturity　n. 期满，到期
12. exchange rate; rate of exchange　汇价，兑换率
official rate　官方汇率
nominal rate　挂牌汇率，名义汇率
spot rate; current rate　现汇汇率
T.T. rate; telegraphic transfer rate　电汇汇率
13. negotiation of draft　汇票交割/汇票议付
14. to receive remittance　收到汇款
15. to make out a receipt　填写收据
16. mode of payment　付款方法
17. payment in full; full payment　付清；支付全部货款
18. payment in arrear　延滞付款
payment in advance; prepayment　预付
deferred payment　延付货款
prompt payment; immediate payment　立即付款
delay in payment; extension of payment　延期付款
payment by installments　分期付款

19. to clear off; to pay off　结清
20. draw (a draft) on sb.　向某人出具汇票
21. down payment　定金
22. deposit　v. 押金

Supplementary Reading

Methods of Payment in International Trade:

1. Open Account (O/A) 赊账(贸易)；记账交易；赊购；赊销

This is the least secure method of trading for sellers, but the most attractive to buyers. It can only be used when sellers are confident that payment will be received.

2. Advance Payment 预付

This is the most secure method of trading for sellers but the least attractive to buyers.

3. Collection 托收

This method is more secure than open account but less so than a letter of credit. There is no guarantee of payment from the bank although it is involved.

a. Documents against Payment (D/P)付款交单

1) D/P at sight

Paying procedure under D/P at sight

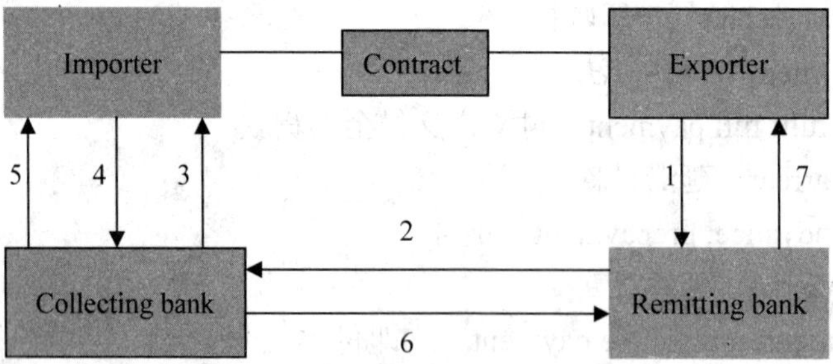

Explanations:

(1) After shipment, the exporter applies to the remitting bank for collecting the invoice value by sending an application, a sight bill and shipping documents to the remitting bank.

(2) The remitting bank draws up a collection order and transfers it as well as the sight bill and shipping documents to the collecting bank.

(3) The collecting bank presents the draft and shipping documents to the importer according to the instructions in the collection order.

(4) The importer pays the purchase price at sight to the collecting bank.

(5) The collecting bank delivers the documents to the importer.

(6) The collecting bank transfers accounts to the remitting bank.

(7) The remitting bank transfer the accounts to the principal.

2) D/P after sight

Paying procedure under D/P after sight:

(1) After shipment, the exporter applies to the remitting bank for collecting the invoice value by sending an application, a time draft and shipping documents to the remitting bank.

(2) The remitting bank draws up a collection order and transfers it as well as the time draft and shipping documents to the collecting bank.

(3) The collecting bank presents the draft and shipping documents to the importer and the importer accepts the draft.

(4) The importer pays in due course to the collecting bank.

(5) The collecting bank delivers the documents to the importer..

(6) The remitting bank transfers the accounts to the principal.

3) Documents against Acceptance (D/A)

Paying procedure under D/A

(1)After shipment, the exporter applies to the remitting bank for collecting the invoice value by sending an application, a time draft and shipping documents to the remitting bank.

(2) The remitting bank draws up a collection order and transfer it as well as the time draft and shipping documents to the collecting bank.

(3) The collecting bank presents the draft and documents to the importer. After the importer accepts the draft, the bank will deliver the shipping documents to the importer, while taking back the draft.

(4) The importer pays the purchase price in due course.

(5) The collecting bank transfers accounts to the remitting bank.

(6) The remitting bank transfers account to the principal.

b. L/C

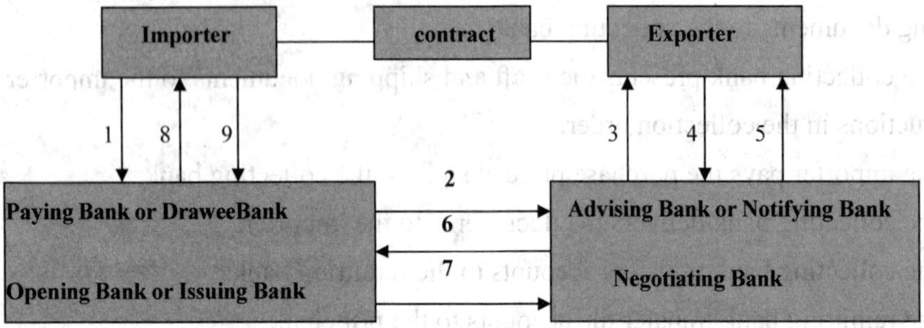

L/C is a reliable and safe method of payment, facilitating trade with unknown buyers and giving protection to both sellers and buyers. The buyer shall open through a bank acceptable to the Seller an irrevocable sight L/C or L/C at … days' sight to reach the Seller ×× days before the month of shipment, and remain valid for negotiation in China until the 21st day after the time of shipment. Paying procedure under L/C：

(1) The issuance of a L/C starts with the buyer who instructs his bank to open a credit (issue an L/C) in favor of the seller for the amount of the purchase.

(2) The buyer's bank (opening bank) sends the L/C to its correspondent in the seller's country, giving instructions about the amount of the credit, the beneficiary, the currency, the documents required and other special instructions.

(3) Upon receipt of the L/C, the correspondent advises the seller of the same immediately.

(4) The seller deals with the correspondent bank and prepares for the shipment of the buyer's order.

After shipment, the seller presents the relative shipment documents to the bank, which should be clearly marked with 'On board M.V xxx' together with a bill of exchange drawn on the opening bank.

(5) The correspondent bank pays the money to the seller when documents presented are found to be in order.

(6) The correspondent bank then sends all the shipping documents to the buyer's bank.

(7) The opening bank pays.

(8) The buyer's bank passes all the shipping documents to the buyer.

(9) The buyer finally reimburses the correspondent bank through the buyer's bank.

Exercises

I. Fill in the blanks with the appropriate words.

(1) We are writing to inform you that your L/C No.1234 opened ______ Standard Chartered Bank should be mended ______.

(2) We have received your L/C No.336 ______ our Sales Confirmation No. 4789. We find that the price terms CIF have been mistakenly indicated as CFR. Please refer ______ the said contract and ______ the amendment ______.

(3) The time of shipment is approaching. Please ______ the L/C as soon as you can.

(4) We consider it ______ to make it clear that for future transaction CAD can only be accepted if the amount ______ is below US$ 3,000 or its ______ in RMB ______ the conversion rate then ______.

(5) According to the contract the blouses will be packed ______ assorted colours.

(6) We are glad to inform you that we have opened an irrevocable L/C No. 465 ______ your favour ______ US$ 4,000 ______ Barclays Bank plc, London, ______ until December 3rd.

(7) As the amount of the transaction is less than US$ 3,000, we wish to ______ payment ______ D/A basis.

(8) The L/C authorizes you to ______ at sight ______ the Bank after shipment is made.

(9) Goods ______ Contract No. 112 were dispatched yesterday.

(10) We have written to you ______ two occasions in the last two months ______ the establishment of the relevant L/C.

(11) ______ examination of the credit, we find transshipment and partial shipments are not allowed.

(12) Please ______ shipment and validity of the L/C ______ July and August 20th ______ with the amendment ______ us by June.

II. Fill in the blanks of the following letter.

Dear Mr. Causio,

Thank you for your letter of May 25th _______for a _______ in payment terms.

After careful consideration with my colleagues, we have come to the decision that it is now time to _______ the business between our two firms. In order to do this, we think an _______ mode of payment could be very helpful. So we propose that for each transaction, when the goods are ready for shipment, we fax you and you pay us 30% of the total value _______ T/T, after _______ which we will _______ the goods and fax you a copy of the Bill of Loading. The rest of the proceeds then will have to be _______by T/T within 20 days of shipment.

We hope this arrangement will be _______to you and will lead to the increase of trade _______ between us.

Yours truly,

III. Translate the following into Chinese.

(1) We can certainly agree to D/P terms, but the international financial market is not stable at the moment; therefore, we think it will be safer for us to handle the business on L/C basis.

(2) We have drawn on you for this amount at sight through the Chartered Bank, who has been instructed to hand over the documents against your acceptance of the draft.

(3) We will accept the goods in three shipments and you may draw on us at 60 d/s from the day of each shipment.

(4) To meet each other halfway, what do you say to 50% by L/C and the balance by D/P?

(5) We have received your cheque for EURO15, 000 in payment for the carpets orders as per your letter of May 25th.

IV. Translate the following into English.

(1) 我们不允许无限期拖欠款项，期望这几天内收到你方上述金额的支票。

(2) 考虑到我们之间长期令人愉快的业务关系，我们同意延期 30 天的信用证支付。相信这将满足你方的愿望。

(3) 我们一贯以信用证方式做业务，希望你方理解我们的处境。

(4) 请注意，宽松的付款条件不但有助于本次交易的顺利进行，而且将会带给双方长久满意。

(5) 我们希望重申一下，我们破例接受 D/P 方式付款仅仅是表明我们与你方发展今后业务的良好愿望。

V. Writing.

Points to be covered in L/C amendment.

(1) Point out the discrepancies or the things you cannot accept.

(2) Give the reasons why the credit should be amended.

(3) Tell the buyer exactly how you want to have the L/C amended.

(4) The time you expect the amendment to arrive.

Unit 8 Insurance

Objective

- Understanding and writing the letters connected with insurance
- Reading and understanding the relative documents

Requirement

- Get a knowledge of the relative documents
- Grasping the usual usage of professional words and sentences
- Grasping the professional terms of insurance

Introduction

Cargo insurance protection is an aid to commercial negotiations. It allows traders to proceed with confidence in the knowledge that each party of the transaction is properly protected. Basically, anyone who has insurable interest in a cargo shipment, i.e. anyone who would suffer a loss if the goods were damaged or destroyed or who would benefit from the safe arrival of the cargo, has a need for ocean cargo insurance. One of the reasons for this is the fact that ocean shipments are still exposed to a number of hazards. Damage or loss of cargo is, however, still a real possibility from such causes as heavy weather, tsunami, earthquake, fire, stranding, collision, moisture, theft, etc.

Insurance for international trading includes Overland Transportation Insurance, Air Transportation Insurance, Parcel Post Insurance and Marine Insurance. However, in most cases, Marine Insurance is of prime importance because the great majority of international trading cargoes are delivered by sea.

Specimen Letters

1. Asking for CIF Terms and Reply

a. Asking for CIF Terms

Dear Sirs,

Referring to our Order No. 90, which is the 3, 000 pairs of men's shoes, we wish to make it place on a CIF basis.

We shall be pleased if you will arrange to insure the goods against All Risks for 110% of the invoice value, i.e., US$ 28, 000.

We sincerely hope that our request will meet with your approval.

Look forward to your early reply.

Yours faithfully,

b. Reply

Dear Sirs,

In reply to your letter of April 11, we are very glad to inform you that we usually make deals on CIF basis, and your requirements could also be met sufficiently. If you still have any demands, please feel free to let us know.

Your close cooperation in this respect is highly appreciated.

Yours faithfully,

2. Request for Excessive Insurance and Reply

a. Request for Excessive Insurance

Dear Sirs,

Considering our deal is based on CIF clause and the products are valuable. W.P.A coverage is too narrow for a shipment of this nature, please extend the coverage to include TPND.

We sincerely hope that our request will meet with your approval.

Look forward to your early reply.

Yours faithfully,

b. Reply

Dear Sirs,

We have carefully considered your order of June 11th, and very glad to inform you that we would take out the coverage of TPND. We always have our customers' interest in mind. If you still have any demands, please feel free to let us know.

Your close cooperation in this respect is highly appreciated.

Yours faithfully,

3. Asking for Additional Insurance and Reply

a. Asking for Additional Insurance

Dear Sirs,

Re：the Order No.070519 for 5,000 Pairs of Men's Shoes

Thank you for your letter of May 17th, 2007, having insured the captioned shipment on our behalf against All Risks for US $28,000 at our cost.

But having in mind the special character of the goods, we shall be pleased if you will arrange to insure the goods on our behalf against Import Duty Risk besides All Risks.

I'm looking forward to your prompt reply.

Yours faithfully,

b. Reply

Dear Sirs,

Re: The Order No.070519 for 5,000 Pairs of Men's Shoes

Thank you for your letter of May 18th, 2007, asking for us to cover the insurance of the captioned shipment against Import Duty Risk besides All Risks for your account.

We have insured the above shipment with the People's Insurance Company of China against All Risks and Import Duty Risk for 110% of the invoice value according to your demand. The policy is being prepared and will be forwarded to you by the end of this week together with our debit note for the premium.

Should you need any other help, please feel free to let us know. We hope we will have a good cooperation on this line in the future.

Yours sincerely,

4. Covering Insurance for the Buyer

Dear Sirs,

Re: The Order No.070517 for 5,000 Pairs of Men's shoes

We are pleased to confirm receipt of your letter of May 15th, 2007, asking for covering insurance of the captioned shipment for your account.

We have insured the above shipment with the People's Insurance Company of China against All Risks for 110% of the invoice value, i.e., US$ 28,000.The policy is being prepared and will be forwarded to you by the end of this week together with our debit note for the premium.

For your information, the goods will be shipped by S/S" East Wind", sailing on or about June 20th.

Yours sincerely,

5. Asking the Buyer to Cover Insurance

Dear Sirs,

Re: Your Order No.070501 for 5,000 Pairs of Men's Shoes

We are pleased to inform you that the Order No. 070501 for 5,000 Pairs of Men's Shoes has been ready now. Since the business is concluded on FOB basis, the insurance should be arranged by you.

For your information, the goods will be shipped not later than May, 2007 by S/S "East

Wind" and they will reach you at the later part of June. So you can cover insurance for the goods.

Should you need any other information, please feel free to let us know.

Best wishes.

Yours sincerely

Relative Documents

1. Insurance policy

中 国 太 平 洋 保 险 公 司 CHINA PACIFIC INSURANCE COMPANY LIMITED 保 险 单 INSURANCE POLICY 填制提单号次 POLICY NO.TB701581 中 国 太 平 洋 保 险 公 司 (以 下 简 称 本 公 司) THIS POLICY OF INSURANCE WITNESSES THAT CHINA PACIFIC INSURANCE COMPANY OF CHINA(HEREINAFTER CALLED "THE COMPANY") 根 据________________ AT THE REQUEST OF________________ (以 下 简 称 被 保 险 人) 的 要 求 ， 由 被 保 险 人 向 本 公 司 缴 付 约 (HEREINAFTER CALLED "THE INSURED") AND IN CONSIDERATION OF THE AGREED PREMIUM PAID TO THE COMPANY BY THE 定 的 保 险 ，按 照 本 保 险 单 承 保 险 别 和 背 面 所 载 条 款 下 列 INSURED UNDERTAKES TO INSURE THE UNDERMENTIONED GOODS IN TRANSPORTATION SUBJECT TO THE CONDITIONS OF THIS POLICY 特 款 承 保 下 述 货 物 运 输 保 险 ， 特 立 本 保 险 单 AS PER THE CLAUSES PRINTED OVERLEAF AND OTHER SPECIAL CLAUSES ATTACHED HEREON 标 记 包 装 及 数 量 保 险 货 物 项 目 保 险 金 额 MARKS & NOS QUANTITY DESCRIPTION OF GOODS AMOUNT INSURED AS PER INVOICE NO. US$ 131,170.00 BF-80285 1000 CARTONS BICYCLES 总 保 险 金 额：USD ONE HUNDRED THIRTY ONE THOUSAND ONE HUNDRED AND EIGHTY ONLY

保 费 费 率 装 载 运 输 工 具

PREMIUM RATE as arranged PER CONVEYANCE SS. ShangCheng V.11

开 航 日 期 自　　至

SLG. ON OR ABT. as per bill of lading FROM SHANGHAI TO YOKOHAMA

承 保 险 别:

CONDITIONS

ALL RISKS AND WAR RISK AS PER PICC

DATED 1/1/2002

本 保 单 项 下 之 保 险 责 任 最 迟 于 货 物 装 船 时 生 效.

THE COVER IS EFFECTIVE AT THE LATEST FROM THE DATE OF LOADING ON BOARD.

所 保 货 物，如 遇 出 险，本 公 司 凭 本 保 险 单 及 其 他 有 关 证 件 给 付 赔 款 。

CLAIMS, IF ANY, PAYABLE ON SURRENDER OF THIS POLICY TOGETHER WITH OTHER RELEVANT DOCUMENTS

所 保 货 物，如 发 生 本 保 险 单 项 下 负 责 赔 偿 的 损 失 或 事 故，

IN THE EVENT OF ACCIDENT WHEREBY LOSS OR DAMAGE MAY RESULT IN A CLAIM UNDER THIS POLICY IMMEDIATE NOTICE

应 立 即 通 知 本 公 司 下 述 代 理 人 查 勘 。

APPLYING FOR SURVEY MUST BE GIVEN TO THE COMPANY'S AGENT AS MENTIONED HEREUNDER:

YEWPEA INSURANCE CO.

12TH FL., URONEY PLAZA

YOKOHAMA, JAPAN

THE CREDIT NO：UCB/JR/268/98 DATED：08-Nov-02

ISSUING BANK：UNITED COMMERCIAL BANK LTD. JUBILEE ROAD BRANCH

赔 款 偿 付 地 点

CLAIM PAYABLE AT/IN YOKOHAMA 中国太平洋保险公司上海分公司

日 期　　　上 海 CHINA PACIFIC INSURANCE CO. LTD. OF CHINA

DATE 11-Jan-01 SHANGHAI SHANGHAI BRANCH

General Manager

地址：中国上海中山南路 56 号 TEL：3234305 3217466-44 TELEX：33128 PICCS CN.

ADDRESS：56 ZHONGSHAN NAN LU ROAD, SHANGHAI, CHINA.

2. Certificate of Insurance

<table>
<tr><td rowspan="2">GERLING KONZERN

ALLGEMEINE
VERSICHERUNGS-AKTIENGESELLECHAFT</td><td colspan="3">Certificate of Insurance</td></tr>
<tr><td>Agency</td><td>Open Cover</td><td>Number</td></tr>
<tr><td>Address of Agency</td><td colspan="3">GERLING SERVICE NEDERLAND N.V.
Herengracht 520, 1017 cc Amsterdam / The Netherlands
Tel.: (20)5249213
Telefax: (20)6268093
Telegrams: Gerlingnet</td></tr>
<tr><td colspan="4">This is to certify that under the above-named open cover insurance is granted to

ORDER

For account of whom it may concern.

Sum insured: USD123,046(USD one hundred twenty three thousand forty six only)</td></tr>
<tr><td colspan="4">Insured goods</td></tr>
<tr><td colspan="4">DEMINERLIZED WHEY POWDER</td></tr>
<tr><td>Gross weight:
Net weight:
Shipping marks:

Packing:</td><td colspan="3">121 380.00 kgs
119 000.00 kgs
CH/99/66.908

DALIAN CHINA
476 025kg in 4-ply paper sacks with inner polyethylene liner and big bags in 7×20′ containers as per contract No. CH/99/66.908 and as per LC No. LC8230074/99</td></tr>
<tr><td colspan="4">Insured Voyage</td></tr>
<tr><td>Place of commencement of insurance</td><td colspan="3">To</td></tr>
</table>

Interior of Helsinki Finland	Dalian, P.R.C.
Via Rotterdam the Netherlands	By means of transport With m.v. Sea Nodica and Lindoe Maersk Shipping date September 15, 1999
Conditions	
1. Marine Insurance (ADS) and Special Conditions for Cargo (ADS Guterversicherung 1973) 2. Conditions of the above-mentioned open cover. 3. From the conditions overleaf the following are applicable. 9, 10, 11 4. Cover applies to the voyage between the places of commencement and termination of insurance mentioned above as per Warehouse to of _____ days after discharge from the ocean vessel at the part of destination. 5. In addition: claims payable in China in currency of the draft, covering ocean marine transportation All risks, War risks. Claims are payable to the bearer. The certificate is made out in 3 originals. If a claims is paid against one of them the other(s) with be void.	
Important instructions to be followed in case of loss or damage see overleaf.	
Claims Survey Agent (to be called in when claims exceed the amount of DM2000.- or counter value in other currency) Huatai Insurance Agency & Consultant Service Ltd. 115 Sidalin Road Dalian China Tel: (411)2654528, 2630872 Fax: (411)2804558 Telex: 86222 picc cn	Date September 12, 1999 GERLING KONZERN ALLGEMEINE VERSICHERUNGS-AKTIENGESELLSCHAFT

Notes

1. tsunami n. 海啸
2. insurable interest 可保利益
3. stranding n. 搁浅
4. collision n. 碰撞
5. Overland Transportation Insurance 陆路的运输保险
6. Parcel Post Insurance 包裹邮寄保险
7. Marine Insurance 海上货物运输保险
8. referring to, speak of,allude to 谈及到，提及
9. insure v. 保险

   the insurer 承保人，保险人，保险公司

   the insured 投保人，进出口交易中为货载投保的买方或卖方
10. deal n. agreement, n. 协议；(尤指)交易

    make/conclude/close/finalize a deal with sb. 与某人达成一笔交易
11. caption n. 标题

    captioned shipment 标题货物
12. on one's behalf as the representative of or spokesman for sb; in the interest of sb

    做某人的代表或代言人；为某人之利益
13. debit note 索款通知
14. premium n. 保险费
15. for one's account 由某人承担
16. PICC People's Insurance Company of China 中国人民保险公司
17. Various kinds of risks：

    the principal perils 基本险

    FPA(Free From Particular Average) 平安险

    WPA 水渍险

    all risks 一切险

    war risk 战争险

    additional Risks 附加险

general additional risks 一般附加险

theft, pilferage & non-delivery(TPND) 偷窃、提货不着险

fresh of shortage 短量险

fresh water/rain damage (FWRD) 淡水雨淋险

risk of intermixture &contamination 混合玷污险

risk of leakage 渗漏险

risk of clash & breakage 碰损破碎险

risk of odor 串味险

damage caused by heating & sweating 受热、受潮险

hook damage 钩损险

loss for damage by breakage of packing 包装破损险

risk of rust 锈损险

special additional risks 特殊附加险

strike risk 罢工险

on deck risk 舱面险

import duty risk 进口关税险

reject risk 拒收险

aflatoxin risk 黄曲霉素险

failure to deliver risk 交货不到险

Exercises

I. Fill in the blanks with prepositions and then translate the following into Chinese.

(1) We shall provide insurance coverage ______ your cost.

(2) Insurance is to be covered ______ the buyers.

(3) They have insured the above shipment with the PICC______ All Risks and Import Duty Risk for 110% of the invoice value according ______ your demand.

(4) A trader can not insure ______ a risk which can not be calculated, such as shoes which suddenly go ______ ______ fashion and which no one wants to buy.

(5) We therefore had the case opened and the contents examined ______ a local insurance surveyor ______ the presence of the shipping company's agents.

(6) Since the premium varies with the extent of insurance, extra premium is ______ the buyers' account should additional risks be required.

II. Fill in the blanks of the following letter.

Dear Sirs,

Re：Our Order No.101 for 5,000 Pairs of Men's Shoes

We wish to refer you ______ our Order No.101 for 5,000 pairs of men's shoes, from ______ you will see that this order is placed ______ a CFR basis.

As we now desire to______ the shipment insured ______ your end ,we shall be pleased if you will arrange to ______ the goods on our behalf ______ All Risks for 110% of the invoice value , i.e., US$ 28, 000.

We shall refund you the premium ______ receipt of your debit note or, if you like, you may draw on us at sight ______ the amount required.

We sincerely hope that our request will meet ______ your approval.

Yours faithfully,

The Ali Trading Corp.

(Signature)

Manager

III. Choose the appropriate words to fill in the blanks.

unsound; against; charges; consignment; claim; covered; recompensed; request; desire; delayed; arrived

(1) The buyers have lodged a claim against the sellers for loss caused by ______ packing.

(2) You may ______ the amount from the underwriters.

(3) Much to our regret, upon inspecting the ______ we found Art.no.A63 missing.

(4) We fell sorry for the ______ delivery and assure you that we have exerted our utmost to expedite delivery. The goods will have ______ at your port by the end of July.

(5) The PICC ______ premiums at lower rates, so it is to your advantage to have your orders insured with the PICC.

(6) As the order was placed on a CIF basis and you ______ the insurance, we should be grateful if you would take the matter up for us with the insurers.

IV. Translate the following into English.

(1) 保险费将与运费一起加在发票金额之中。

(2) 对于 CIF 的交易，我们一般按发票金额的 110%投保一切险。

(3) 我方很遗憾的告诉你方，由“××”轮运来的货物的状况令人十分不满，我们不得不向你方提出索赔。

(4) 如果要求更高的百分率，我们也能照办，但你们必须承担额外的保险费。

(5) 你方索赔需要有充分的证据，由中国商检局出具的检验报告将作为最后的依据，对双方都有约束力。

(6) 如果货物发生损坏，你方可在货到达目的港 30 天内凭公证行的检验报告与你处保险代理行联系并向他们提出索赔。

V. Translate the following into Chinese.

(1) Please let us know immediately the detailed risks you wish to insure against for your shipment in question. In the absence of definite instructions from our clients, we generally cover WPA.

(2) We have insured all future shipments of hand tools made by you from your warehouse in Tianjin to our warehouse in London under an open policy for the total amount of US$ 100,000. If the value of any shipment exceeds this figure, we shall make adjustment accordingly.

(3) As our insurance company is a state-operated enterprise enjoying high prestige in settling claims promptly and equitably, you are advised to do business with us on CIF basis and leave the insurance to be effected by us.

(4) According to our usual practice, insurance is to be effected for 110% of the invoice value.

(5) For goods sold on CIF basis, insurance is to be effected by us for 110% of the invoice value against All Risks based on warehouse to warehouse clause.

(6) The premium varies with the extent of insurance. Should additional risks be covered, the extra premium would be for buyers' account.

VI. Writing.

Write a letter, replying the enquiry of offering Insurance Coverage. Tell them according to the usual practice, this kind of commodities is covered by FPA. If they require having their shipment against other risks, the extra premium will be on their account.

Supplementary Reading

Insuring Your Shipment

When shipping to a foreign market, cargo insurance is strongly recommended. It is essential if the terms of sale require the exporter to arrange for insurance, for example a C.I.F contract (cost, insurance, freight). In any event, the cost of cargo insurance is nominal in most cases, amounting to less than 1% of the value of the shipment and the freight bill.

With the proper insurance policy, exporters can recover losses if their shipments are accidentally lost, stolen, damaged or delayed, although the extent of recovery will depend on the type of insurance purchased. Without insurance, an exporter could have no recourse. Unfortunately, insurance does not cover the possible loss of a customer, who may shift to another source of supply because the goods ordered do not arrive in a usable condition or are late in arriving.

When buying insurance, the exporter should consider several things, such as the amount of coverage (all risks or limited), time of year, route and destination port (the North Atlantic during the winter months can be treacherous; some ports can have higher than usual rates of pilferage), the loss and damage record of competing carriers, and cargo stowage and packing.

Insurance should be viewed as part of the total rate and service package that the carrier (or forwarder) offers, so don't treat insurance in isolation. Even though a carrier may have an impeccable record, there is always an element of risk and exporters should protect themselves against this risk.

Moreover, insurance coverage is part of a carrier's marketing strategy. It is more than likely that cost, coverage and the number of loss and damage claims will vary from carrier to carrier, so ask several and compare. Ask the carrier, whether it is a rail, motor, marine or intermodal carrier, what it charges for insurance, what the insurance covers, the deductible (if any) and how claims are handled.

This suggests that the first step in insurance selection is to ask the carrier about its loss and damage record. Ask other exporters or, if you are a member of an organization such as the Canadian Industrial Transportation Association, ask if it has any record on a particular carrier.

Before exporting, make clear that the terms of sale specify who is responsible for arranging insurance. For example, an exporter selling "C.I.F." will be responsible for arranging and paying for freight insurance. In many transactions, it is common for Canadian exporters, even those selling "F.O.B." or "F.A.S.", to control or arrange for marine insurance.

Which kind of insurance the exporter should buy depends on the mode of transport selected, as certain levels are established according to legal requirements. Railway carriers are completely responsible for loss and damage to cargo. Motor carriers are responsible for \$2.00 per pound, but will provide full coverage for a fee of 1% of the value of the load. Ocean carriage is limited to \$500 per package, which is frequently below the value of the shipment. Consequently, the exporter must arrange for coverage separately. Exporters should be aware that there certain are exceptions which override the carrier's liability, such as "Acts of God" or a defect in the goods.

Obviously, for highway/ocean shipments or intermodal shipments moving partly by a marine carrier, full coverage may require the purchase of separate insurance from each carrier. For shipments that involve ocean carriage, it is recommended that exporters include an "all risks" clause.

Insurance can be arranged directly with a carrier, an insurer, an insurance broker or agent or through a freight forwarder or customs broker. Whether you purchase from a carrier or a third party, make sure that the insurance purchased covers the entire journey, that is from the time it leaves your plant or warehouse until it is in the importer's warehouse. In some instances, a carrier will provide coverage only while it is handling the shipment.

It should be noted that this discussion is meant for shipments of general freight and for lost or damaged cargo. Insurance for products such as dangerous goods and hazardous wastes are covered by separate insurance regimes. Responsibility for issues such as cleanup costs in the event of an accident involving your goods is not covered.

Unit 9 Complaint, Claim & Settlement

Objective

- Understanding and writing the letters connected with complaint, claim & settlement

Requirement

- Grasping the usual usage of professional words and sentences
- Grasping the professional terms of insurance

Introduction

On execution of a sales contract, both parties to the contract must strictly perform their respective obligations. If one of the parties breaches the contract, the other may run into trouble, or suffer great losses. In this case, the affected party is entitled to request the defaulter to make up his losses according to the relevant provision under the contract. The request, which is made by the affected party, is called a "claim", and the party responsible for the losses or damage takes measures to deal with the claim is called "settlement of claim". However, the affected party, in consideration of the good relation with the other party, or the loss incurred being a minor one, sometimes does not lodge a claim against the suppliers, but rather than request him to make sure that such things will not happen again. This is a "complaint" rather than a claim.

Generally speaking, a complaint may arise from any of the following situations:

(1) The wrong goods may have been sent.

(2) The quality may not be satisfactory.

(3) The goods may have been delivered damaged or late.

(4) The prices charged may be excessive, or not as agreed.

When the amount of money involved is large, the party who suffers will lodge a claim against the other for compensation on the strength of a survey report or other official documents supporting the claim.

How does the affected party make his claim so that he gets the best adjustment he desires? A claim letter should be planned as follows:

(1) Begin by regretting the need to complain.

(2) Mention the date of the order, the date of delivery and the goods complained about.

(3) State the reasons for being dissatisfied and ask for an explanation.

(4) Refer to the inconvenience caused.

(5) Suggest how the matter should be put right.

(6) Close courteously with a request for prompt action.

Reply to complaint and claim should always be courteous, even if the complaint or the claim is unfounded; the sellers should not repudiate the claim until they have good and reliable ground to do so.

Suppose you are the seller, the following rules are to be noted when dealing with a claim:

(1) The first thing that has to be decided is whether the claim is justified. If so, then you have to admit it readily; express your regret and promise to put matters right.

(2) If the claim is not justified, point this out politely and in an agreeable manner. It would be a wrong policy to refuse the claim offhand.

(3) If you cannot deal with a claim promptly, acknowledge it at once. Explain that you are looking into it and that you will send a full reply later.

(4) All claims should be treated as serious matters and thoroughly investigated.

(5) The close of the letter should be positive, i.e., with the assumption that all is forgiven and normal relationship can be resumed.

There is no need for the sellers to go into a long story of how the mistake was made and a short explanation may be useful.

Specimen Letters

1. Complaint Concerning Wrong Goods Delivered

Dear Sirs,

Our Order No.1314

We duly received the documents and took delivery of the goods in arrival of s. s. "Seafarer" at Hamburg.

We are much obliged to you for the prompt execution of this order. Everything appears to be correct and in good condition except in Case No.67.

Unfortunately，when we opened this case we found it contained completely different articles, and we can only presume a mistake was made and the contents of this case were for another order.

As we need the articles we ordered to complete deliveries to our new customers, we must ask you to arrange for the dispatch of replacements at once. We attach a list of the contents of case No.67, and shall be glad if you will check this with our order and the copy of your invoice.

In the mean time, we are holding the above mentioned case at your disposal. Please let us know what you wish us to do with it.

Yours faithfully,

2. Complaint for Late Delivery and Reply

a. Complaint for Late Delivery

Dear Sirs,

Re：Our Order No.222, 1000 Sets of Copy Machines

Please note that we have repeatedly requested you by letters to effect shipment in time. To our disappointment, however, we received no response from you before yesterday.

We receive your shipping advice today. But the contracted time of delivery is overdue. You may be aware that your continued silence has placed us in an awkward position. As you failed to make delivery in time, our customers have to turn to other suppliers and we have missed the sales season. Consequently, we have no choice but to cancel our order with you. In the meantime, we reserve the right to lodge a claim on you for our losses incurred.

We have no wish to embarrass you and hope you will understand how we are placed and all possible steps will be taken by you to avoid any recurrence of similar nature in your future dealings.

Yours faithfully,

b. Reply to Complaint for Late Delivery

Dear Sirs,

Re：Our Order No.222, 1000 Sets of Copy Machines

Thank you for your letter regarding your order No.222. We are very much sorry to hear that you have to cancel the order.

Personnel adjustment in our corporation caused the goods delay in delivery, which have brought you inconvenience and losses. We apologize for our faults. You may be rest assured that we will compensate you for the loss caused by our late delivery.

We hope all our efforts can give you a satisfactory reference that we do not want to loss you as our customer.

We look forward to your continuing order.

Yours faithfully,

3. Claim for Inferior Quality and Reply

a. Claim for Inferior Quality

Dear Sir,

After carefully examining the dress materials supplied to our order of June 2nd, we are surprised and disappointed at their quality. Obviously, they do not match the samples you sent us. Some of them are so poor that we cannot help feeling there must have been some mistake in making up the order.

The materials are quite unsuited to the needs of our customers and we have no choice but to ask you to take them back and replace them by materials of the quality ordered. If this is impossible, then we are afraid we shall have to ask you to cancel our order.

We have no wish to embarrass you if you can replace the materials we are prepared to allow the stated time for delivery to run from the date you confirm that you can supply the materials we need.

Yours faithfully,

b. Reply to the Above

Dear Sirs,

We very much regret to learn from your letter of June 20th that you are not satisfied with the dress materials supplied to your order No.886.

From what you say it seems possible that some mistakes have been made in our selection of the materials meant for you and we are arranging for our sales manager in your area, Mr. Zhang, to call on you later this week to compare the materials supplied with the samples from which you ordered them.

If it is found that our selection faulty, then you can most certainly rely on us to replace the materials. In any case, we are willing to take the materials back and, if we can not supply what you want, to cancel your order, though do this reluctantly since we have no wish to lose your customer.

Yours faithfully,

4. Claim for Short-weight and Settlement

a. Claim for Short-weight

Dear Sirs,

Claim for Short-land Fertilizers under S/C No.6543

Further to our fax dated August 26th.

We have just received the Survey Report from the Dalian Commodity Inspection Bureau evidencing the broken bags being due to improper packing for which the suppliers are definitely responsible.

On the strength of the DCIB's Survey Report we hereby register our claim with you as follows:

Our claim on short-delivered quantity	£357.00
Plus survey charges	£25.00
Total amount of claim	£382.00

Survey Report No. TE(06)305 is enclosed and we look forward to your settlement at an early date.

Yours faithfully,

b. Settlement

Dear Sirs,

Your Claim on 1,000 M/T Chemical Fertilizers

With reference to your letter of September 6th, in which a claim was lodged for a short delivery of 1,540 lbs Chemical Fertilizers, we wish to express our deepest regret over the unfortunate incident. You must have had many difficulties in meeting the orders of your clients.

After check-up by our staff at the warehouse in Glasgow, it was found that some 10 bags had not been packed in 5-ply strong paper bags as stipulated in the contract thus resulting in the breakage during transit. This was due entirely to negligence on the part of the warehouse manager for which we, the exporters, tender our apologies.

In view of our long-standing relations of which, we trust, there is a good prospect of further development we will make payment by cheque for £382.00, the amount of claim, into your account with the Bank of China, upon receipt of your agreement.

We hope this matter will not affect our good relations in future dealings.

Yours faithfully,

Notes

1. complaint　n. 诉苦，抱怨，牢骚，委屈，疾病

complain　vt./vi. 抱怨，责难

2. claim

(1) n.(对权利等的)要求，索赔，索款，索汇。通常与动词 lodge，file，make，raise，register，make，put in 搭配使用。索赔对象前常用介词 against，with，或 on；索赔的原因前用 on，for 或 on account of。

如：to lodge/file/enter/register/make/raise/put in a claim against/with sb. on a certain shipment for a certain reason for amount of money…对某批发货由于某种原因向某人提出金额为……的索赔。

(2) vt. 索赔，索汇，索款；要求(应得)权利；声称，主张

(3) vi. 索赔，提出要求

3. survey report　检验报告

4. settlement　n. (争执、纠纷等)解决；(账款)偿付，(账目)结算

5. took delivery of…　提货

6. s. s.　轮船，即 steamer ship 的缩写

7. execution　n. 完成，执行

8. be obliged to sb.　感谢某人

9. replacements　n. 替换，调换；调换的物品，补充的货物

10. at one's disposal　由某人支配/处理

11. place sb. in an awkward position　使某人处于尴尬的境地

12. reserve the right to do sth.　保留做某事的权力

13. make up　v. 弥补，虚构；补足，拼凑

14. rely on　依赖，依靠

15. a short delivery　短交；交货短量，交货短额

16. lbs. = pounds　磅

Exercises

I. Fill in the blanks with proper words or expressions and then translate the following into Chinese.

(1) We are lodging a claim______ the shipment ______ s. s. "Chunlan" ______ short delivery.

(2) We shall remit to you an amount of $ 200 in ______ for the loss you suffered.

(3) Your claim for the damage is to be ______ with the insurance company.

(4) We are sorry to hear that the goods you received are not ______ the quality expected.

(5) We have received many complaints ______ the customers concerning the watches supplied by you under our order No. 22.

(6) Such being the case, we are compelled to ______ the right of lodging a claim ______ you.

(7) We confirm ______ received your remittance______ $650 ______ settlement ______ our claim.

(8) Your claim has been passed on ______ our insurance company, who will get ______ touch ______ you soon.

(9) ______ the time of lodging, the goods ______ in good condition.

(10) Please ______ ______ the matter as one of urgency and let us have your cable reply earlier.

II. Fill in the blanks of the following letter.

Dear Sirs,

Thank you for your letter dated May 20th, in _____ you lodge a claim _____ the faulty operation of the newly delivered copy machine.

We are very much sorry ______ the difficulties you have encountered, and have requested Mr. Su, our sales manager in your city, to call you to ______ a necessary time when he may call on and carry out the effective ______ under the manufacturer's guarantee.

We would like to ______ you that HP range ______ a well-earned reputation for overall reliability in service. I'm, therefore, ______ that once the faulty machine has been adjusted, you will have no further cause for ______.

We trust this unfortunate error will not adversely ______ our future transaction.

Yours faithfully,

III. Choose the appropriate words to fill in the blanks.

by; for; on; after; through; up to; as; upon; in

(1) They made a claim ______ us for the damage.

(2) The shipping company must be responsible ______ the goods damage in transit.

(3) We are sorry to hear that the goods you received are not ______ the quality stipulated in contract.

(4) The goods under Order No. 223 are so badly damaged ______ consequence of careless packing that we can not sell them.

(5) ______ examinations we found that the goods do not agree the original.

(6) Your claim should be supported ______ sufficient evidence.

(7) In view of the long business relations between us, we agree to solve the dispute ______ friendly discussions.

(8) The survey report issued by China Commodity Inspection Bureau will be taken ______ final and binding ______ both parties concerned.

IV. Translate the following into English.

(1) 希望贵方尽快更换错发的商品。

(2) 复验后发现，你方发来的货物质量与合同规定不符。

(3) 买方向船方提出金额为$ 800 的索赔。

(4) 很遗憾，你方发来的货物短装 360 千克。

(5) 请立即处理此事，并注意不可再拖延交货。

V. Translate the following into Chinese.

(1) Please claim on our behalf against the ship-owners who are evidently responsible for the loss.

(2) Claims, if any, should be settled against the survey report from China Commodity Inspection Bureau.

(3) We are unable to accept the shipment which we received from you today, as they had been completely smashed when they reached us.

(4) We enclose our check in amount of $ 3,000 in final and complete settlement of this claim.

(5) Wrongly delivered the goods is the fault of our persons in charge of packing.

VI. Writing .

Write to your suppliers explaining that in a delivery of metal wastepaper bins twenty-eight were slightly dented or badly scratched and you have had to sell them at a price considerably below the recommended retail selling price. Submit a claim for the difference between the recommended retail price and the price at which the damaged bins were actually sold.

Supplementary Reading

a. Useful Sentences

(1) I'm afraid you should compensate us by 5% of the total amount of the contract. 贵公司要赔偿我方合同全部金额的百分之五。

(2) I propose we compensate you by 3% of the total value plus inspection fee. 我想我方赔偿贵方百分之三的损失，另外加上商检费。

(3) We regret for the loss you have suffered and agree to compensate you by US$ 500. 我们对你方遭受的损失深表歉意，同意向你们赔偿 500 美元。

(4) We register a claim for US$ 200. 我们提出索赔 200 美元。

(5) The Australian Company agreed to compensate us for the defective watches by 4% of the total value. 澳大利亚一家公司同意就有缺陷的手表向我们赔偿总价值的百分之四。

(6) Claim on short-weight is caused by packing damage or short-loading. 短重索赔是由包装破损或装运短重引起的。

(7) Claim on delayed shipment is that sellers fail to make the delivery according to time schedule. 延期索赔是对卖方没有按时装运货物而提出的索赔。

(8) Claim on quality originates from inferior quality of goods or quality changes. 品质(质量)索赔是在货物质量低劣或是质量改变的条件下发生的。

(9) As our shipping documents can confirm that the goods were in perfect condition when they left here, and that show they were damaged in transportation. Therefore, we cannot give our consideration to your claim. 由于我们的装运单据能确认货物离开此地时完好无损，显然货物是在运输过程中损坏的。因此，我方不同意你方的索赔。

b. A Practical Case of Claim

A Chinese export company sold 25 metric tons of Donkey Meat to an Australian client. As stipulated in the contract, the goods were to be packed in 1, 500 boxes with a net weight of 16.6 kilos per box. If the goods were packed according to stipulations, the total weight was 24.9

metric tons, the remaining 100 kilos might not be delivered. But, when the goods arrived at Australian port, the Australian client checked them and found that each box contained 15.5 kilos. Therefore, this shipment amounted to 23.25 metric tons. However, the goods totaled 24.9 M/T in weight on all the documents, and the payment was also effected against 24.9 M/T. Thus, there were 1,650 kilos Donkey Meat short delivered. Consequently, a claim was lodged by the Australian client for a short delivery of 1,650 kilos Donkey Meat for amount of US$ 37,950. After examination, the exporter found that the short-delivered goods is due to the fault of the person in charge of packing. So, the exporter had no choice but to compensate for the Australian client.

Unit 10 Agency

Objective

- Understanding and writing the letters connected with agency
- Reading and understanding the relative readings about agency

Requirement

- Knowing the major types of agents
- Grasping the usual usage of professional words and sentences
- Grasping the professional terms of agency

Introduction

It is well known that many transactions in international trade are handled not by direct negotiation between buyers and sellers but by agencies, usually in the country of the buyer. It is more convenient and economical for a foreign trade company to do their buying and selling business through agencies abroad, because a foreign agent is well familiar with the market conditions in which he will operate, and he knows what goods and what prices are best suited to his area.

There are mainly two types of agents: general agent and sole or exclusive agent. A general agent may be a firm or a person who acts under instructions from his principal to sell or buy on the best terms obtainable. He charges a commission for his services under certain agreement or contract. Similar to a general agent, a sole agent, also called exclusive agent, may be a firm or a person who acts for his foreign principal with exclusive agent rights to sell in a certain area on a commission basis certain commodities supplied by the principal under some agreement. The sole agent will not sell other goods that compete with the principal's, and for a general agency there is no such undertaking.

Specimen Letters

1. Application for Agency and Reply

a. Application for Agency

Dear Sirs,

We take the liberty to write you this letter to ask if you are already represented in South Korea, as we are interested in acting as your sole agent for the sale of your bicycles both for adults and for children in our country.

We are one of the largest, long-standing establishments in all kinds of machines. We have better knowledge of the market here and good business relations with the domestic wholesalers and the leading retailers. We visited your stand at Shanghai Bicycle Exhibition the other day. And we think the high quality, attractive design and reasonable prices of your bicycles will appeal to our customers. We feel confident that if you give us any opportunity to deal in your goods, the result will be entirely satisfactory to both of us. We handle a couple of other agencies, but they are in non-competing lines.

As to our financial standing and reliability, we wish to refer you to our bank and the other manufactures which we cooperate with. They will offer you the first-class references that prove us agents of highest integrity.

We are looking forward to your favorable reply.

Yours sincerely,

b. Reply

Dear Sirs,

We thank you for your letter dated March 10th, recommending yourself to be our sole agent for bicycles in South Korea.

We appreciate your offering. However, to be frank, we have to say that it would be premature to consider the matter of agency at this stage when we know a little about your company and your future volume of business.

We are of the opinion that it would be better for both of us to try out a period to see how things go. Also it would be necessary that you build a certain turnover to justify the agency arrangement.

Therefore, we think it advisable to postpone the matter until your future sales warrant such a step. We hope our views will be shared by you and we will make joint efforts to enhance our happy cooperating relationship.

Yours faithfully,

2. Appointing Sole Agent

Dear Sirs,

Sole Agency for Chinese Embroideries in Sweden

We have received your letter of April 15th and are favorably impressed with the proposal you make. After our serious consideration, you are kindly informed that we have decided to appoint you the sole agency for Chinese Embroideries in the territory of Sweden.

The Agency Agreement has been drawn up for duration of one year, automatically renewable on expiration for a similar period unless a written notice is given to the contrary. Enclosed you will find a copy of the draft. Please go over the provisions and inform us whether they meet with your approval.

We shall do all in our power to assist you in establishing a mutually beneficial trade.

Yours faithfully,

3. Confirmation of Agency Terms of Sole Agent

Dear Sirs,

It is our pleasure to learn from your letter of September 10th that you are willing to entrust us with your sole agent for marketing Chinese Embroideries in Sweden.

We have gone over the detailed terms in your Agency Agreement and now confirmed them as follows:

(1) That the agency commences on January 1st, 2008 and is terminated on January 1st,2009, subject to renewal.

(2) That the agency is a sole agency for marketing Chinese Embroideries in Sweden.

(3) That we undertake not to handle competing products of other local manufacturers while the sole agency agreement remains in force.

(4) That you pay us quarterly a commission at 5% based on the total sales of your goods in Sweden.

(5) That all accounts are settled at the end of each year.

(6) That we keep a full range of your products in our showrooms.

It will be appreciated if you send us the formal Agency Agreement at your earliest convenience.

Yours faithfully,

Notes

1. agency　n. 代理处(可数)；代理关系，代理，代理权(不可数)

代理在法律上指一人授权另一人代理他行动的关系。前者叫委托人(principal)，后者叫代理人(agent)。

sales agent　销售代理人
purchasing agent　采购代理人
sole (exclusive) agent　独家代理人
commission agent　佣金代理人
manufacturer's export agent　厂家出口代理人
general agent　总代理人
advertising agent　广告代理人
shipping agent　运输代理人
insurance agent　保险代理人

2. act as … 充当……
3. establishment n. 公司，企业组织
4. have good knowledge of… 很好地了解，掌握……
5. appeal to… 对……有吸引力，投其所好
6. confident adj. 有信心的，确信的(多用作标语，后接 of 或 that 从句)
7. non-competing lines 非竞争性系列产品
8. as to… 关于(可接用名词或名词从句)……
9. financial standing 财务状况
credit standing 资信情况
10. refer sb. to sb. for sth. 请某人与某人商洽某事
We refer you to your insurance company for recovery of this fee.
请你们与你方保险公司商洽，要求赔偿这笔费用。
11. integrity n. 诚实；正直；信誉
business integrity 商业信誉
12. premature adj. 未成熟的，过早的；过快的，草率的
13. at this stage 目前，暂时
14. moderate adj. 中等的，适度的
15. be of the opinion that… 认为，相信，主张(后接 that 连接同位语从句，该句式语体较 think 正式庄重)
16. justify vt. 证明……是正当的、正确的或有效的
justification 不可数名词，意思是“正当的理由”
17. advisable adj. 可取的，明智的(常用做表语或补语)
18. warrant vt. 证明……为正当，成为……的条件或证据，与 justify 同义
19. postpone the matter 推迟此事
20. be impressed with… 被……所打动
21. territory n. 领土，版图，地域
22. Agency Agreement 代理协议
23. renewable adj. 可恢复的，展期的
24. unless a written notice is given to the contrary 除非另有书面通知
25. meet with your approval 得到你方认同
26. do all in our power to do sth. 竭尽全力做某事
27. a mutually beneficial trade 互利贸易
28. entrust sb. with… 委托某人
29. market v. 销售，推销

30. approve　vt. 批准，同意(后直接加名词或动名词做其宾语)

31. draft　n./v. 草稿，草案；设计，起草

32. commence　v. 开始

terminate　v. 终止

33. subject to renewal　重新续签后生效

34. manufacture　v./n. 制造，加工；制造业，产品(常用复数形式)

manufacturer　n. 制造业者，厂商

35. undertake　v. 保证，同意，许诺(后接 that 从句或动词不定式)

36. in force　有效，实行

come into force　开始生效，开始实行

Exercises

I. Choose the best answer to complete each of the following sentences.

(1) We wish to ________ as an agent the goods you are exporting now, because we are commanding an extensive domestic market in this line.

A. deal　　B. handle　　C. import

(2) Having acquired much experience in marketing products similar to yours, we are ________ with customer's needs and are confident we could develop a good market for you in our region.

A. familiar　　B. familiarize　　C. familiarized

(3) We are convinced that there is a profitable market in our area waiting to be tapped for your products and we should like to ________ as your agent in this line.

A. take　　B. set　　C. act

(4) In view of your past efforts in pushing the sales of our products, we have decided to accept your proposal to ________ you our agent in China.

A. entrust　　B. appoint　　C. act

(5) After paying due consideration and investigating your business standing, we decided to entrust you ________ the sole agent for Chinese Tea in the territory of North America.

A. of　　B. for　　C. with

(6) With a view to developing business, most disputes ________ in carrying out contracts can and should be solved in an amicable manner.

A. involve B. involved C. involving

(7) This agreement, when duly signed by the parties concerned, shall remain ________ force for two years.

A. in B. to C. for

(8) If you are interested in our proposal, please let us know which of our products are most likely to appeal ________ your customers.

A. by B. to C. of

(9) If you confirm these terms we will arrange for a formal agreement to be ________ up.

A. draw B. drawing C. drawn

(10) Both sides must stick ________ the stipulations of the agreement.

A. to B. with C. in

II. Choose the appropriate words to fill in the blanks.

worthwhile; basis; line; appoint; view; appreciated; with; convinced; agency; for

Dear Sirs,

In________ of the steady increase in the demand ________ our beauty preparations (shampoo, lipsticks, etc.), we have decided to ________an agent to handle our export trade with your country.

From our own observations and the experiences of competitors, we are ________ that there is an enormous market potential waiting to be tapped, and that a really active and efficient agent could develop a fine business in this ________. As we think you are the right person to do this, we would like to offer you the________ if you are at all interested, and we should welcome your views.

We offer a sole agency, and would supply you ________ a reasonable initial stock on the ________ of credit of 6 months. Further supplies would be invoiced to you at 10% below export list prices, with payment by quarterly draft.

An early reply would be ________, as we wish to reach a quick decision. Meanwhile we hope you will see in our offer a ________ opportunity.

Yours faithfully,

III. Translate the following into Chinese.

(1) Please be assured that we would do all we can to support you as far as your sales territory is concerned.

(2) Your commission, based on your turnover, will be 2%.

(3) After a period of two years the agreement may be cancelled at any time without prior notice.

(4) Thank you for your confidence. I am ready to accept your representation in your country.

(5) I must decline because the conditions offered are not acceptable.

(6) I suggest the agency contract should be initially made for a trial period of one year.

(7) If the agent wishes to work for other firms as well, he must obtain our permission first.

(8) We will reimburse the expenses of the advertising for the representative.

(9) If there is evidence of a breach of contract by either party, the contract may be cancelled immediately. Cancellation of the contract must be made in writing by registered mail.

(10) The question of agency is still under consideration and we hope that you will continue your efforts to promote the sales of our products.

IV. Translate the following into English.

(1) 如有偶然的经济事件发生时，本代理契约可经双方同意，做部分的修改。

(2) 如果本协议的部分被违反，并不意味着整个协议的终止。

(3) 所应支付的佣金必须按月寄给代理人。

(4) 广告费用由本契约的双方当事人平均分担。

(5) 代理人在被指定的地区内担当职务，他的活动仅限于此地区内。

(6) 我们已经草拟了一份代理协议，请查阅，并确认协议的细节。

(7) 我们应坦率告知，鉴于目前你方成交额不大，考虑代理事宜尚为时过早。

(8) 感谢你方提议让我们担任贵公司产品的独家代理，我们深信，我们的合作将会为贵方的出口产品提供更多的机会。

V. Translate the following letter into English.

尊敬的执事先生：

从贵国驻华盛顿大使馆的商务参赞处欣获贵公司地址。多年来我们经营纺织品，并对销售贵公司产品颇感兴趣。

目前我们是本地区和邻近国家几家知名公司的代理，平均销售业绩甚佳。我们雇用了优秀的业务员，同时有足够的仓储设备和运送用的大卡车。

假如贵公司愿意把美国东部地区的代理由我们来承揽的话，我们确信必能为你们提供更多的业务。

期待回复。

某某谨上

2007年4月15日

VI. Writing

Write a letter to entrust a customer with agency, with the following given particulars.

(1) 7月6日来函收悉。经过认真考虑，已决定委托贵商行为我方独家代理，负责在加拿大销售我方的园艺机械工具。

(2) 代理协议现已拟妥，期限一年。期满时若无废约通知，即再自动生效一年。

(3) 随函附寄协议草稿一份，请详阅其条款，并请惠告是否同意。

(4) 为建立互利贸易，我方将尽力协助你们。

Supplementary Reading

International trade is rather complicated because there are obstacles and differences in terms of currency, measurement systems, commercial laws, trade customs and habits, tariffs, transportation and insurance of goods, and other artificial obstacles. Therefore, it is important to choose and appoint an agent who is familiar with local conditions and the market and can operate the business to mutual benefit. In modern market economy, considerable transactions are conducted by agencies.

1. The definitions of Commercial Agent, Broker and Salesman

Commercial Agent

The commercial agent negotiates and concludes contracts on behalf of his principle. Although the degree of his independence from the principal varies, he is never totally independent.

Broker

The broker is a business agent who is completely independent of his principal. The broker negotiates sales and purchase contracts for importers and exporters, but he / she does not have the right to the ownership of the goods.

Salesman

This type of agent is a dependent employee of a merchant who concludes contracts for the merchant outside the business establishment. Salesman usually draws a certain percentage of commission on each sale.

2. What the principal should do, prior to the appointment of an agent

Before appointing an agent the principal should make a careful investigation about experience and professional morality of the firm or the person to be appointed, such as:

(1) The reliability and financial soundness of the prospective agent.

(2) His marketing and sales promoting skills.

(3) His market connections and sales channels.

(4) Whether the prospective agent is also an agent of similar goods.

3. Contents of an Agency Agreement

The terms and conditions of agency should be made clear and definite before the agreement is signed by the parties concerned. Points to be covered in the agreement may include the following:

(1) The principal and the agent

(2) The nature and duration of the agency(e.g. general agency, exclusive agency or sole agency; a buying agent for importer)

(3) The territory to be covered

(4) The products the agent is appointed for.

(5) The commission for the agent

(6) The rights and duties of the agent and the principal.

(7) The method of purchase and sale (e.g. the agent is to buy on his own account or on consignment).

(8) Details of expenses to be allowed such as for the faxes and telephone calls.

(9) The method of arbitration in case of the event of dispute.

Unit 11 Compensation Trade, Processing & Assembling Trade

Objective

- Understanding and writing the letters connected with compensation trade
- Reading and understanding the processing and assembling trade related contracts

Requirement

- Get a knowledge of compensation trade, processing & assembling trade
- Grasping the usual usage of professional words and sentences
- Grasping the professional terms of compensation trade, processing & assembling trade

Introduction

Compensation trade is a form of counter trade in which incoming investment is repaid from the revenues generated by that investment. In compensation trade, a Chinese enterprise conducts production by using the technology, equipment, and certain raw materials, if necessary, provided by an overseas supplier or the technology and equipment introduced into China by means of foreign export credit. The Chinese enterprise will pay off the cost of the technology, equipment and raw materials or the loans and their interests thus incurred by selling the manufactured goods back or by amortization with its income from processing.

Compensation trade should be conducted with the focus on accelerating technological innovation in the industry of the country and expanding its production of commodities for export so as to increase the country's foreign exchange income. Generally, there are two kinds of compensation trade, i.e. direct compensation trade (buyback) and indirect compensation trade (counter purchase).

Processing and assembling trade refers to the business activity of importing all or part of the raw and auxiliary materials, parts and components, accessories, and packaging materials from abroad in bond, and re-exporting the finished products after processing or assembly by domestic enterprises. It includes processing with supplied materials and processing with imported materials.

Under processing with supplied materials, the imported materials and parts are supplied by the foreign party which is also responsible for selling the finished products. The business enterprise does not have to make foreign exchange payment for the imports and only charges the foreign party a processing fee. Under processing with imported materials, the business enterprise makes foreign exchange payment for the imported materials and parts and exports the finished products after processing.

Specimen letters

1. Proposal for Compensation Trade and Reply of Agreement

a. Proposal

Dear Sirs,

We thank you very much for your hospitality to our delegation last month. We were pleased to take the opportunity to discuss the possibilities of importing the machines and equipment from you on the basis of compensation trade.

In compliance with our discussion, we shall repay the cost of the machines and equipment with the steel wire ropes processed with the said machines and equipment in 4 lots within two years after the trial operation of the machines. The price of these steel wire ropes is to pay for the machines and equipment you supply plus insurance and freight. Our bank will open an irrevocable banker's acceptance L/C in your favor to cover the machines and equipment. The L/C will become valid after we receive your irrevocable sight L/C in our favor for equal amount of the resultant products within one week.

The above-mentioned points are the principles on which the compensation trade agreement is to be constituted. Should the above be found acceptable to you, please let us know immediately so that we can negotiate further and bring the transaction to an early successful conclusion.

We await your early reply.

Yours faithfully,

The Global Import & Export Co., Ltd.

b. Reply

Dear Sirs,

We are pleased to learn from your mail of March 6th that you will consider compensation trade arrangements for the supply of our machines and equipment and up to now, we fully agree to your proposal.

As requested by you, we have made out a draft agreement with all the necessary terms and conditions for your consideration. Should you have any different views on the provisions, please do not hesitate to communicate with us.

Your early reply will be highly appreciated. We are looking forward to cooperating with you in the near future.

Yours faithfully,

Messrs. Carlson & Marwell

2. Processing and Assembling Trade

a. Processing Trade

Dear Sirs,

Thank you for your letter of June 22nd inquiring about the possibility of manufacturing Leather Bags with supplied materials and according to your samples.

As one of the leading leather products manufacturers and exporters in China, we have been doing business of processing according to supplied samples and processing with supplied materials for years, in addition to our ordinary import and export transactions. Our leather products are superior in materials and excellent in workmanship. You can be assured that the processing and delivery of the leather bags will prove to your full satisfaction.

Enclosed please find our counter-sample, on which basis we quote our processing fee for each piece at US$XXX, including the cost of all accessories. Delivery can be expected within two months after receipt of your materials.

We assure you of our close co-operation at any time and look forward to receiving your reply at an early date.

Yours sincerely,

b. Assembling Trade

Dear Sirs,

Your Vice President had several pleasant and fruitful discussions with us about assembling refrigerators while he visited Shanghai early this month. Now we wish to mention the following four points as supplements to the previous discussions.

(1) With the components, auxiliary materials, and necessary equipment and tools supplied by your company, we shall assemble 36,000 refrigerators within a period of three years, namely, 8,000 domestic refrigerators and 2,000 industrial refrigerators to be assembled within the first year (2006), 10,000 domestic refrigerators and 3,000 industrial refrigerators to be assembled in the second and the third year respectively.

(2) All the finished products will bear a neutral brand. 60% of the finished products will be shipped to Hong Kong and 40% to Sydney. Shipment of the products is to be effected once half a year. All the shipping expenses will be for your account.

(3) Payment for the assembling fee and shipping expenses is to be made by sight L/C to be opened by you not later than 30 days before the shipping schedule.

(4) In case there arise some disputes which couldn't be solved, it is necessary to state an arbitrator who can settle such disputes. Unless otherwise agreed, contracts are commonly governed by the laws of our country.

Please give the above points your careful consideration. Your early reply will be highly appreciated.

Yours faithfully,

Relative Documents

COMPENSATION TRADE CONTRACT

No.________________

This Contract made on April 20th 20_ _, at ______, China, between The Global Import & Export Co., Ltd. with its principal office at ______, China (hereinafter called Party A) , and Messrs. Carlson & Maxwell with its principal office at______, USA (hereinafter called Party B) ,Whereas Party B has machines and equipment, which are now used in Party B's manufacturing of steel wire rope, and is willing to sell to Party A the machines and equipment, and Whereas Party B agrees to buy the products, steel wire rope, made by Party A using the machines and equipment Party B supplies, in compensation of the price of the machines and equipment, and Whereas Party A agrees to purchase from Party B the machines and equipment, and Whereas Party A agrees to sell to Party B the products, the steel wire rope, in compensation of the price of Party B's machines and equipment; Now therefore, in consideration of the premises and covenants described hereinafter, Party A and Party B agree as follows:

1. Purchase Arrangement

Party A agrees to purchase from Party B the following commodity under the terms and conditions set out below:

(1) Commodity, Specifications and Its Capability

Commodity:

Specifications:

Capability:

(2) Quantity:

(3) Price: On FOB ___ basis.

Unit Price: US$XXX ; Total Price: US$XXX.

(4) Payment:

Party A shall, within 15 days after signing this Agreement, establish in favor of Party B an irrevocable Banker's Acceptance L/C in payment for the machines and equipment, for an amount not less than US$ XXX, available by draft at 180 days sight. The irrevocable L/C will be effective only after receipt by Party A of a satisfactory reciprocal L/C opened by Party B for payment of the steel wire rope.

(5) Shipment：

Time of shipment：

Port of loading：

Port of destination：

Shipping marks：

(6) Insurance：

To be effected by Party A.

(7) Inspection：

(8) Guarantee：

Party B guarantees that the machines and equipment are un-used, sophisticated and of best quality, and that the machines and equipment are capable of manufacturing the steel wire rope (_________ specifications with a production of _________meters per hour).

2. Sales Arrangement

Party A sells to Party B the steel wire rope in compensation of the price of the machines and equipment Party B sells to Party A.

(1) Commodity and Specifications：

Commodity：steel wire rope.

Specifications：

(2) Quantity：

________meters of steel wire rope per year, of which the price shall be ________US Dollar annum.

(3) Price：

The price of the steel wire rope shall be set on the basis of the prevailing price in the world market at the time when shipment is made. The price shall be based on CIF basis.

(4) Payment：

From the date of acceptance of the draft and not later than 7 days thereafter, Party B shall reciprocally establish in favor of Party A an irrevocable L/C in payment for the steel wire rope, for an amount not less than US$XXX, available by sight draft. The L/C shall be in strict accordance with the terms and conditions of this agreement. Otherwise, Party B shall be held responsible for the delay in shipment and Party A may lodge claims against Party B for the losses arising therefrom. All the expenses arising from the amendments shall be for Party B's account.

(5) Shipment:

Shipment shall be made twice a year, in June and in December, each for the value of ________.

Port of loading:

Port of destination:

Shipping marks:

(6) Packing:

To be packed in wooden reels.

(7) Insurance:

To be covered by Party A for 110% of the invoice value, covering W. P. A. and War Risk.

(8) Inspection:

The quality certificate issued by Party A shall be regarded as final. If, on arrival of the goods at the port of destination, Party B finds the quality not up to the specifications mentioned above, Party B shall notify Party A within 45 days after arrival of the goods at the port of destination. Both Parties shall have consultations for a settlement of the matter in dispute.

3. Force Majeure

Party A or Party B shall not be held responsible for any failure or delay in delivery of the entire lot or a portion of the goods under the contract as a result of any force majeure accident (s).

4. Arbitration

All disputes arising in connection with this contract or in the execution thereof, should be settled amicably through negotiations. In case no settlement can be reached, the case in dispute shall then be submitted for arbitration in ________. The decision of the arbitration shall be accepted as final and binding upon both parties.

This agreement is written in Chinese and English versions. Both versions are equally authentic. In the event of any discrepancy between the two aforesaid versions, the Chinese version shall prevail. INWITNESS WHEREOF, the parties have executed this agreement in quadruplicate by their duly authorized representatives as of the date first above written.

Party A: Party B:

__________ __________

(signature) (signature)

Notes

1. compensation trade　补偿贸易

指在信贷基础上进口机器设备，然后用引进的机器设备生产的产品或其他产品或劳务，分期偿还进口设备的价款及利息。

2. hospitality　n. 好客，殷勤；款待客人

The people of your company showed me great hospitality.

你们公司的人对我非常殷勤好客。

3. delegation　n. 代表团

In the last few years, more and more foreign business and trade delegations have come to China for business.

过去的几年里，越来越多的外国企业和贸易代表团来华发展贸易。

delegate　n. 代表

We have authorized Mr. Roy Smith as our delegate to discuss the particulars of the compensation trade agreement with you.

我们已经授权 Roy Smith 先生作为我方代表，与你方讨论有关补偿贸易协议的具体细节。

delegate　vt. 授(权)，把……委托给

We have delegated our New York Branch to attend to all your orders.

我们已委托纽约分公司处理你方所有订单。

4. compliance　n. 依从，遵守；顺从，听从

in compliance with　与……一致

In compliance with your request, we are sending a quotation together with a range of pamphlets for your reference.

按照你方要求，我们奉送报价单一份，并附一套小册子，供你方参考。

5. repay　v.　偿付，偿还

We will repay the outstanding amount chiefly with the products produced by the machine.

我们主要用该机器生产的产品来偿付余下未付款项。

repayment　n. 偿付，偿还；偿还的款项

Repayment will be made quarterly without bearing any interest.

偿付款每季度支付一次，不带利息。

6. lot n. 一批货

The goods are to be shipped in three lots of 20 metric tons each on separate bills of lading.

货物分三批装运，每批 20 吨，提单分开。

7. trial operation 试运转

8. an irrevocable banker's acceptance L/C 不可撤销银行承兑信用证

9. valid adj. 有效的

We regret to learn that you have not been able to make a valid effort to push this line.

我们遗憾的获知，你方推销此类货物未能生效。

validity n. 有效，效力，正确

After another week, the credit will lose its validity.

再过一周，信用证就将失效。

10. irrevocable sight L/C 不可撤销即期信用证

11. resultant product 直接产品

You should hold yourselves responsible for buying back or pushing sales of the resultant products produced with the said machine.

你们应负责返销或推销该机器生产的直接产品。

12. constitute v. 制定，构成

His action constitutes a breach of contract.

他的行为构成了违约。

They are gathering comments from people in all walks of life to constitute new traffic regulations.

他们收集各类人群的意见，以便制定新的交通法规。

13. negotiate v. 商议，磋商，谈判

14. bring sth. to a conclusion 达成；使……结束

With mutual efforts, we have finally brought the business to a conclusion.

通过共同努力，我们最终达成了这笔业务。

15. make out 起草

We will make out a draft of the sales contract based on our previous negotiation.

我方将在前期的磋商的基础上起草销售合同。

16. draft n. 草稿，草案，草图

Please include the same Arbitration Clause in the draft agreement you are to prepare.

请在你方准备的协议草案中，包括同样的仲裁条款。

17. terms and conditions　条款，条件

We are very pleased to learn that the terms and conditions we agreed upon had been finally approved by your company.

很高兴得悉我们双方商定的条款最终获得你公司批准。

18. provision　n. 规定

Both sides have to act according to the provisions of the agreement.

双方都应该按照协议条款办事。

19. processing trade　加工贸易

指从国外进口全部或部分原料、辅件、零件或包装材料，利用本国设备和劳动力，加工成成品再出口的贸易方式。包括来样加工和来料加工两种形式。

processing according to supplied samples (designs)　来样加工

processing with supplied materials　来料加工

processing fee　加工费

process　v. 加工；处理

We can assure you that the raw material will be carefully processed.

请放心，我们会认真加工这些原料。

We will process your order as soon as possible.

我们会尽快处理你们的订单。

process　n. 过程，步骤

The manufacture of your order is in process.

你方的订货正在生产中。

20. accessory　n. 辅料；(机器的)附件

We can assure you that you will have the finished products six months after the fabric and accessories arrive here.

我们保证在面料、辅料到达六个月后，你们就会拿到成品。

21. assemble　v. 组装，装配

They assemble the parts and components into a car.

他们把零部件装配成一辆汽车。

assembling with supplied parts and components　来件装配

Exercises

I. Fill in the blanks with the missing words given below and then translate the following into Chinese.

end; capital; operation; assembly; compensation; technology; resultant; raw; parts; processing

________ and ________ differ from Compensation Trade or Buyback Arrangements in that we already posses the skill, know-how and ________ equipment necessary for ________, and normally, not ________ transfer takes place. In ________ trade we pay for the cost of technological imports by delivery of ________ products, otherwise, called ________ goods. In the type of processing or assembly deal, we charge a fee for processing of ________ materials or assembly of ________. Therefore, this type of trade is beneficial to us and likely to be expanded in the future.

II. Choose the appropriate words to fill in the blanks.

(1) In compensation trade, we pay for the cost of technological imports by delivery of end products ________ in processing or assembly deals, we charge a fee for processing raw materials or assembly of parts.

A. while B. when C. whether D. if

(2) After expiration of the contracted period of two years, the supplied equipment and tools will become our property ________.

A. with charge B. free charge C. uncharged D. free of charge

(3) All parts and components made in Shanghai must ________ the standards of quality, and be approved by Part A beforehand.

A. add up to B. measure up to
C. be measured up to D. be made of

(4) Party B undertakes to compensate Party A for the contract amount by exporting ________ cartons of Canned Pear.

A. in two lots B. in two lot C. with two lots D. with two lot

(5) In case the delivered value of feather exceeds that of machinery equipment, Party B shall ship such additional spare parts as indicated by Party A to ________ the difference.

A. get off B. set off C. get up D. set up

(6) Party B shall establish in favor of Party A an irrevocable Banker's Acceptance L/C in payment ________ the equipment ________ an amount not less than HK$ 22 million.

A. of … for B. to … for C. for … at D. for … for

(7) The factory was awarded the contract for the ________ with supplied drawings.

A. processing Gear Boxes B. processings of Gear Box

C. process of Gear Box D. processing of Gear Boxes

(8) We don't need the exact total right now; an ________ figure will suffice.

A. approximate B. rough C. gross D. estimated

(9) There is a ________ that your quality products will sell well in our city.

A. possibility B. credit C. consideration D. potential

(10) If you find a compensation trade acceptable, please don't ________to tell us.

A. hesitate B. regret C. notify D. submit

III. Translate the following into English.

(1) 机器的价款可以用由此生产出来的产品作价支付，整个交易可按补偿贸易方式进行。

(2) 我们愉快地获悉你方同意在补偿贸易的基础上出售塑料喷射机。

(3) 进口的生产资料和技术的费用将主要由用它们生产出来的产品分期偿还。

(4) 你方提供技术和设备，而我方提供厂房，劳动力和其他合作生产所需的资源。

(5) 考虑到我们的友谊和未来的生意合作，我们同意按来料加工的方式加工童装。

(6) 我方工厂已完成返销产品中的900套，其余的正在制造中。

(7) 最近我们已开始承担来料加工业务，材料全部或部分由客户提供。

(8) 30台缝纫机的成本将由我方预付，并由你方分期偿还，外加运费和每年2%的利息。

(9) 他们将把这些配件组装成成品并运到你方指定的港口。

(10) 我方可以按照指定品牌进行来料加工。

IV. Translate the following into Chinese.

(1) We wish to stress that the equipment and technologies provided by you should be up to standard, suitable for our production and reasonable in price.

(2) The products used for compensation in principle shall be the products directly produced with the imported equipment and technologies. If necessary, however, upon mutual consent, other products can also be used for repayment.

(3) Repayment of the cost of the imported capital goods will be made by installments with the products thus manufactured.

(4) On the basis of credit, compensation trade can be divided into tow types according to the method of payment.

(5) Our main objective of doing compensation trade is to import advanced equipment and technology.

(6) Processing trade means to have parts of machines and appliances processed and assembled.

(7) We grant you the right to use our trademark upon the authorized products assembled by you.

(8) Earning processing fee is not the sole object of our accepting orders for processing with supplied materials.

(9) Here is a copy of the specimen of processing trade contract with all the related terms and conditions.

(10) We suggest that you accept our countersale products each year to a value not less than our installment payment to you in the same year.

V. Writing.

Write a letter to Messrs. Bill Simpson & Co., accepting compensation trade arrangement for the import of production line and the export of electrical appliance. Give the quotation and the information about the delivery of the resultant products. Add any other conditions you may think of.

Unit 12 Joint Venture & Tender

Objective

- Understanding and writing the letters connected with joint venture and tender
- Reading and understanding the relative contracts and documents

Requirement

- Getting a knowledge of the relative documents
- Grasping the usual usage of professional words and sentences
- Grasping the professional terms of joint venture and tender

Introduction

A Joint Venture is a business arrangement in which the participants create a new business entity or official contractual relationship and share investment and operation expenses, management responsibilities, and profits and losses.

The Chinese authorities encourage foreign investors to run company in this form in order to obtain exposure to advanced technology and new management skills. In return, foreign investors can enjoy low labor costs, low production costs and a potentially large Chinese market share. Profit and risk sharing in a joint venture are proportionate to the equity of each partner, except in case of a breach of the joint venture contract. There are 2 types of joint venture： equity joint venture and contractual joint venture.

A tender is an offer or proposal to purchase a special quantity of a commodity for a specified price. The international plant-engineering contract is a comprehensive international cooperation in economy and technology, including machines and equipment, technology, capital and service, under which one party (the contractor) shall undertake the responsibility of fulfilling the building of a certain project item, and the other party (the employer) shall offer necessary working conditions and give the acceptance to the project, and pay the agreed amount of the price value and the service reward. Generally, a tender involves the procedures as invitation for bids, submission of tenders, bid opening, tender discussion and tender decision, establishment of contract, and execution of contract.

Specimen letters

1. Joint Venture

a. Proposal

Dear Sirs,

We are one of the largest manufacturers and exporters of chemical fertilizer in the world, having over 30 years' experience in this line of business. We have factories producing chemical fertilizers not only in practically all the industrials cities in our country but also cities in many other countries.

We are pleased to learn that China is encouraging joint ventures with foreign firms and favorable terms will be given to those who are enthusiastic about promoting economic and technical cooperation with China. We take this opportunity to approach you in the hope that you will introduce to us any Chinese partners who are interested in forming joint ventures with us in the manufacture of the chemical fertilizers in China either for domestic use or for export.

It is understood that joint venture involves complicated legal procedures as well as arrangements relating to the percentage of contributions, distribution of dividends and management, etc., of which we should like to hear full details from you so that we may go further into the matter.

We hope our participation in forming a joint venture with Chinese partners will make a small contribution to China's modernization in chemical industry. We look forward to your early reply.

Yours faithfully,

b. Reply

Dear Sirs,

Thank you for your letter of September 20th, expressing your desire to set up a joint venture to manufacture chemical fertilizers in China.

We have immediately contacted some of the potential Chinese partners, who show their interest in the participation but first of all they would like to know the approximate amount of your investment and in what form your contribution will be, i.e. in cash, capital goods or technology. They would also like to know where you prefer to locate the project site.

To pave a flexible and smooth way for foreign investment, the Chinese government has promulgated the law on equity joint venture and the law on contractual joint venture, which provide that:

(1) The proportion of investment by foreign investors in a joint venture should not be less than 25% with no top limit.

(2) The profits and risks should be shared in proportion to the partners' respective contributions in an equity venture while in a contractual joint venture, everything is done as contracted.

(3) The joint venture will be run under the guidance of the board of directors. The number of directors as well as each party's rights and responsibilities should be determined on the basis of the investment that they have made in the business.

Detailed information is included in the enclosed copies.

China keeps providing an excellent investment environment and preferential treatment to foreign investors, which have attracted a lot of foreign investments. We believe that, through our joint efforts, our prospective joint venture will prove successful.

Yours faithfully,

Encl. a/s

2. Invitation for Bid

AURORA CONSTRUCTION CORPORATION
INVITATION TO BID
UTILITY TRUCK

We invite you to bid on the anticipated purchase of one utility truck.

Sealed Bids will be received at the office of …at 2: 00 p.m., local time, on Wednesday, March 29th, 20_ _ to determine proposals for the anticipated purchase of the above named project.

Attached please find specifications and other pertinent documents necessary for you to respond to this Bid invitation.

Each Bid must be placed in an envelope, sealed, and clearly marked on the outside: "Bid for Utility Truck".

Prospective bidders must call-in their interest in this Invitation to Bid with our Purchasing Division at phone No.×××giving a name, address, phone and e-mail address in order to receive any possible addendum information. Failure to do so may subject bidder to disqualification.

Aurora Construction Corporation reserves the right to reject any or all Bids, or parts thereof, and to waive any technicality, informality or irregularity in the Bids received, and to disregard all nonconforming or conditional Bids or counter-proposals and to hold the best Bids for ninety (90) days from the opening date set forth above. The Corporation further reserves the right to award the Bid to the lowest responsible Bidder whose offer best responds in quality, fitness and capacity to the requirements of the proposed work or usage and therefore is in the best interest of the Corporation.

AURORA CONSTRUCTION CORPORATION

Bruce Lawrie
Purchasing Director

3. Letter of Submission of Bid

Re：Request for proposals of__________, 200__ concerning the sub-project________________.

After having read the bidding documents relating to the above-mentioned works and in particular the following four documents：

(1) Instructions to bidders;

(2) Draft contract;

(3) Form of estimated quantities;

(4) Specifications and drawings;

On behalf of my company, I hereby:

(1) Accept, without restrictions, all the provisions in the Bidding Documents;

(2) Submit a contract price bearing my signature and completed by me following the mode that was sent to me;

(3) Agree, as the Contractor, to carry out the works named below, following the provisions of the price list; and

(4) Submit a draft contract bearing my signature.

The Executing Agency (Employer) shall pay the amounts due from it and set forth in the detailed work statements, by crediting the bank account opened in the name of：______________________, number__________________, at the __________________branch of the_________ Bank, or in cash against witnessed receipts.

Done in one original copy

at______ on _________200__

Signed by_________________

The Contractor

Name of the company_______

Address and telephone_______

Relative Documents

1. Notice of Invitation for Open Tender

Notice of Opening Invitation to Bid

(Tender No：7279SU10)

(1) Technical specifications and technical performances for required equipment are defined in the Tender Documents.

(2) Interested parties can collect the Tender Documents at ______, between 09:00 and 15:00hrs local time, every working day starting from the date of the last announcement. The closing date for collection of the Tender Documents is 15 working days from the date of the last announcement.

(3) Tender documents will be handed over to Bidders who have confirmed in writing (i.e. by e-mail or facsimile) their interest to participate at the Employer's address/facsimile number indicated below.

(4) Each Bidder is allowed to submit only one Proposal and only in English language. Only complete Proposals will be accepted.

(5) All Bids must be submitted to _________, within 52 days from the date of the last announcement, 12:00hrs. local time. Late submissions will not be taken into consideration.

(6) The price of the tender documents is 100 Euro. This amount must be transferred to ________ - Account No.____________. Payments by foreign Bidders must be made in EURO as follows：

Bank：____________________

SWIFT BIC：________________

BANK ACCOUNT OF THE NATIONAL BANK OF _____

IN ______, - ______.

(7) Public opening will take place at _________, 3 working days after the closing date of the Tender, at 10:00hrs local time.

(8) For any further information, please contact the following telephone/facsimile, e-mail address:

2. Bid bond

KNOW ALL PERSONS BY THESE PRESENTS:

We, ______________________________________, as "Principal,"

(Name of Principal)

and_________________________, an____________ Corporation,

(Name of Surety)

authorized to transact Surety business in ______, as "Surety," hereby jointly and severally bind ourselves, our respective heirs, executors, administrators, successors and assigns to pay unto ____________ as Obligee, the sum of (US$_________)_________________________________ dollars.

WHEREAS, the condition of the obligation of this bond is that Principal has submitted its proposal or bid to an agency of the Obligee in response to Obligee's procurement document (No. ____________________) for the project identified as: _______________________ _____________________which proposal or bid is made a part of this bond by reference, and Principal is required to furnish bid security in an amount equal to ten percent (10%) of the total amount of the bid pursuant to the procurement document.

NOW, therefore, if the proposal or bid submitted by Principal is accepted, and if a contract pursuant to the proposal or bid is awarded to Principal, and if Principal enters into and executes such contract within the time specified in the Instructions to Bidders and executes and delivers to Obligee its good and sufficient Performance Bond and Payment Bond required by Obligee within the time fixed by Obligee, then this obligation shall be void; otherwise, it shall remain in full force and effect.

IN WITNESS WHEREOF, we have caused this instrument to be executed and sealed by our duly authorized legal representatives this ________________day of _______________________, 20____.

PRINCIPAL: ______________ SURETY: _______________

By: __________________ By: _________________

Title: ___________________ Title: ____________________

3. Qualification of Certificate

BIDDER'S CERTIFICATION

I, __________(Name) of _________________(Bidder's name and address) a bidder proposing to furnish the following described materials, equipment, and/or services to XXX Corporation.

Hereby certifies that:

(1) Bidder has thoroughly inspected the specifications or request for proposal and understands the terms and conditions thereof and they are incorporated by reference in the bid or proposal for said goods or services, and has verified measurements.

(2) The bid or proposal is firm and binding and shall be valid for not less than sixty (60) days from the date of bid opening. A longer time may be set out in the bid, or negotiated between the Bidder and the Corporation.

(3) The bid or proposal is made by a person authorized to bind the bidder.

(4) The bid or proposal is made without unlawful collusion with the Bidder or potential bidder or with any officer or employee of the Corporation.

(Signature of person making affidavit): ______________

Notes

1. Joint venture　合资企业

   equity joint venture　合资经营企业

   contractual joint venture　合作经营企业

2. complicated legal procedures　复杂的法律程序

3. percentage of contributions　捐资比例；摊款比例

   contribution　n. 贡献；促进；捐款；投资；出资

4. distribution of dividends　利润分红，红利分配
distribution　n. 分配；配给物
5. modernization　n. 现代化
6. participation　n. 参加，参与
7. pave a way for　为……铺平道路
8. promulgate　vt. 颁布；公布
9. proportion　n. 比例；部分；(复数)大小
10. top limit　上限
11. board of directors　董事会
12. profits and risks　盈利和风险
13. share　v. 分担，分享
share　n. 股份；份额
14. preferential treatment　优惠待遇
15. joint efforts　共同努力
16. invitation to (for) bid　招标
bid　n. 投标
bidder　投标人
17. anticipate　v. 预期；期望
18. sealed bid　密封标书
19. cutaway utility truck　公用载重汽车
20. division of electrical maintenance　电器维修部
21. pertinent　adj. 有关的，相干的
22. call-in　打电话
23. addendum information　附录信息
24. disqualification　n. 无资格，取消资格
25. waive　vt. 放弃；取消
26. irregularity　n. 不规则，无规律
27. disregard　vt. 不理会；忽视，忽略
28. nonconforming　adj. 非一致性的
29. conditional bids　有条件的投标
30. set forth　宣布，提出
31. award　n., vt. 裁决
award of bid　决标　win the award　中标

32. submission of bid　投标
33. bidding documents　投标文件
34. on behalf of　作为……的代表
35. restriction　n. 限制，约束
36. contractor　n. 订约人，承包人
37. carry out　完成，执行
38. due　adj. 应付的，所欠的
39. credit　vt. 记入贷方，贷记
40. witnessed receipts　见证人收据

Exercises

I. Choose the appropriate words to fill in the blanks.

(1) We have agreed to _____ a joint venture company in that developing country.

A. put forward　　B. set up　　C. put up　　D. open

(2) We have noticed the British producers _____ a joint venture agreement with Chinese companies.

A. interest in　　B. are interested in

C. are interested　　D. interest

(3) The party _____ shall appoint 3 directors.

A. that have 70% shareholding　　B. have 70% shareholding

C. with 70% shareholdings　　D. having 70% shareholding

(4) We should be obliged if you could furnish us _____ a detailed report _____ the financial position, business lines and other aspects of the joint venture.

A. with, on　　B. with, for　　C. on, for　　D. for, on

(5) The joint venture should apply for the extension of the term _____.

A. six months expiration before　　B. before expiration six months

C. before six months expiration　　D. six months before expiration

(6) The two firms agree to ____a joint venture in China.

A. enter into　　B. intend　　C. engage　　D. embark on

(7) According to international practice, bidders need to _____ cash deposit or letter of guarantee from the bank when bidding.

A. hand out　　B. hand over　　C. hand in　　D. hand on

(8) This bid is _____ for a period of 120 calendar days from the date of the bid opening.

A. validity B. validate C. validation D. valid

(9) The judge _____ a large sum of money to the seller as damages.

A. forwarded B. awarded C. rewarded D. warded

(10) If you are interested in _____ a bid, please contact the Purchasing office for a copy of the specifications.

A. offer B. give C. submit D. transfer

II. Translate the following into English.

(1) 我们很高兴得知贵公司希望与我方在澳大利亚成立批发服装合资企业。

(2) 合资企业的业务是进口和批发我国生产的布匹和其他纺织品。

(3) 所有企业利润、亏损、成本和债务将按各方的持股比例分摊。

(4) 中国的政策是与外国企业和公司建立合资企业以扩大国际经济合作和技术交流。

(5) 你们合资企业的注册资本是多少？

(6) 我们准备就该项目向国际招标。

(7) 我公司欢迎国内外企业投标建设核发电站。

(8) 有关该项招标详细内容要求，如需进一步了解情况，请函询×××。

(9) 投标截止日期为北京时间 2006 年 4 月 30 日下午 4 时寄到上述地址。

(10) 各项投标文件，均须为经正式签署的正本，并经密封后寄出。

III. Translate the following into Chinese.

(1) China promises that it's the country's basic policy to open up to the outside world and attract foreign investment.

(2) We'd like to know what procedures should be taken to engage in a joint venture with you.

(3) Joint Venture will help China import advanced and appropriate technology, acquire useful experience in management and train qualified personnel.

(4) The Chinese Government protects in accordance with The Law of the Investment of Foreign Joint Ventures.

(5) All the activities of a joint venture shall comply with the provisions of the law, decrees and pertinent regulations of the People's Republic of China.

(6) Bidders should have the needed technical knowledge, great experience and enough financial power.

(7) Your bids will not be considered if you fail to furnish a bid bond before the opening of

bid.

(8) Bidders shall send all the documents required by the Tendering Corporation in one lot before the closing date to participate in the bid.

(9) The result of the tendering is that the contract is awarded to YYY Corporation with the second lowest bid, but not to XXX Corporation with the lowest bid.

(10) All bids from foreign corporations must be submitted by their representative offices registered in Shanghai.

Supplementary Reading

Useful Sentences

(1) We appreciate the contributions you have made to the marketing of this article.
我们感谢你方在推销此商品上所作的贡献。

(2) Our contribution will be partly in cash and partly in equipment.
我们的投资一部分是现金，一部分是设备。

(3) Distribution and consumption are two major subjects in Political Economics.
分配和消费是政治经济学的两大主要课题。

(4) The success of the deal depends on the participation of all parties concerned.
交易的成功取决于有关各方的参与。

(5) A number of laws and regulations have been promulgated with respect to the establishment of joint venture.
我们已经颁布了一系列有关设立合资企业的法律法规。

(6) The parties to the joint venture shall share the profits, risks and losses in proportion to their respective contributions to the registered capital.
合资各方依其注册资本投资的比例分享利润，分担风险及亏损。

(7) Shall we each invest 50% capital and share the profit equally?
我们双方是否可以各出资一半，并平均分配盈利？

(8) Their share of trade in Asian market has amounted to 60%.
他们在亚洲市场的贸易中所占的份额已达到60%。

(9) Many companies bid on the new bridge and only the one that bids the lowest price will win the contract.
许多公司参加这座大桥的投标，只有标价最低的才能中标。

(10) The bidders are anticipated to face keen competition.

预计投标者将面临激烈的竞争。

(11) Please make the entire pertinent documents necessary ready for the bid.

请把投标需要的所有相关文件准备好。

(12) They agree to waive all rights to any claim against the company.

他们同意放弃对该公司可主张任何要求的权力。

(13) Disregarding all difficulties, we succeeded in bringing them around in the end.

我们不顾一切困难,终于说服了他们。

(14) The report addresses in great deal the distinction between the acceptable and unacceptable nonconforming bid.

报告以很大篇幅说明了可接受的投标与不可接受不一致的投标的区别。

(15) Only the bidder who bids the lowest price and meets the requirements in quality of the proposed project has the possibility to win the award.

只有标价最低，并且满足该项目质量要求的投标公司才有可能中标。

(16) We will grant a license without restriction to the applicant who meets the standard license requirements.

对于符合标准执照要求的申请者，我们将无条件地向其颁发执照。

(17) We have remitted you all the commissions due up to date yesterday.

昨天我们已将迄今为止欠你方的所有佣金汇出。

参 考 文 献

[1] 简怡．新世纪商务英语函电[M]．天津：天津大学出版社，2003.
[2] 曹菱．商务英语函电[M]．北京：外语教学与研究出版社，2000.
[3] 林季红．商业英文书信范例[M]．北京：外文出版社，2004.
[4] 刘志伟．国际商务函电与沟通[M]．北京：对外经济贸易大学出版社，2005.
[5] 戚云芳．外经贸英语函电与谈判[M]．杭州：浙江大学出版社，2003.
[6] 滕美荣，许楠．外贸英语函电[M]．北京：首都经济贸易大学出版社，2005.
[7] 王乃彦．外贸英语函电[M]．北京：中国对外经济贸易出版社，2002.
[8] 兰天．外贸英语函电[M]．沈阳：东北财经大学出版社，2002.
[9] 廖瑛．实用外贸英语函电[M]．武汉：华中科技大学出版社，2003.

21世纪全国应用型本科财经管理系列实用规划教材(已出版)

序号	标准书号	书　　名	主　　编	出版时间
1	ISBN 978-7-5038-4748-6	应用统计学	王淑芬	2007年2月
2	ISBN 978-7-5038-4875-9	会计学原理	刘爱香 贾圣武	2007年8月
3	ISBN 978-7-5038-4881-0	会计学原理习题与实验	齐永忠 贾圣武	2007年8月
4	ISBN 978-7-5038-4892-6	基础会计学	李秀莲 张　华	2007年8月
5	ISBN 978-7-5038-4896-4	会计学原理与实务	周慧滨 王素萍	2007年8月
6	ISBN 978-7-5038-4897-1	财务管理学	盛均全 原晓燕	2007年8月
7	ISBN 978-7-5038-4877-3	生产作业管理	李全喜	2007年8月
8	ISBN 978-7-5038-4878-0	运营管理	冯根尧	2007年8月
9	ISBN 978-7-5038-4879-7	市场营销学新论	郑玉香 刘泽东	2007年8月
10	ISBN 978-7-5038-4880-3	人力资源管理	颜爱民	2007年8月
11	ISBN 978-7-5038-4899-5	人力资源管理实用教程	吴宝华	2007年8月
12	ISBN 978-7-5038-4889-6	公共关系理论与实务	王　玫 王志敏	2007年8月
13	ISBN 978-7-5038-4890-2	服务企业经营管理学	于干千 秦德智	2007年8月
14	ISBN 978-7-5038-4884-1	外贸函电	王　妍 肖　艳	2007年8月
15	ISBN 978-7-5038-4894-0	国际贸易	朱廷珺	2007年8月
16	ISBN 978-7-5038-4895-7	国际贸易实务	夏合群 周英芬	2007年8月
17	ISBN 978-7-5038-4883-4	国际贸易规则与进出口业务操作实务	李　平	2007年8月
18	ISBN 978-7-5038-4885-8	国际贸易理论与实务	缪东玲	2007年8月
19	ISBN 978-7-5038-4873-5	国际结算	张晓芬 李劲涛	2007年8月
20	ISBN 978-7-5038-4893-3	国际金融	韩博印 王学信	2007年8月
21	ISBN 978-7-5038-4874-2	宏观经济学原理与实务	崔东红 何伟平	2007年8月
22	ISBN 978-7-5038-4882-7	宏观经济学	蹇令香 付廷臣	2007年8月
23	ISBN 978-7-5038-4886-5	西方经济学实用教程	陈孝胜	2007年8月
24	ISBN 978-7-5038-4870-4	管理运筹学	关文忠 韩宇鑫	2007年8月
25	ISBN 978-7-5038-4871-1	保险学原理与实务	曹时军 曾玉珍	2007年8月
26	ISBN 978-7-5038-4872-8	管理学基础	于干千 卢启程	2007年8月
27	ISBN 978-7-5038-4891-9	管理学基础学习指南与习题集	王　珍 卢启程	2007年8月
28	ISBN 978-7-5038-4888-9	统计学原理	刘晓利	2007年8月
29	ISBN 978-7-5038-4898-8	统计学	曲　岩 刘继云	2007年8月
30	ISBN 978-7-5038-4876-6	经济法原理与实务	杨士富 刘晓善	2007年8月
31	ISBN 978-7-5038-4887-2	商法总论	任先行	2007年8月